TIME TO REMEMBER,
TIME TO FORGET

MEMOIRS OF THE DEMBINSKI FAMILY

In particular the story of the family's deportation from Poland during the Second World War

by

ANDRZEJ DEMBINSKI

Copyright ©2018

All rights reserved

ISBN-13: 978-1986817974

Contents

Introduction 1
Family Tree - Dembinski Family 4
Family Tree - Plewkiewicz Family 5
The Family Members in this Story 6
CHAPTER 1 7
Prelude to War 7
CHAPTER 2 14
Travellers' Tale - Warszawa to Przemysl 14
    1st September to 8th November 1939 14
CHAPTER 3 29
Przemysl – The Frontier that Never Opened 29
    8th November 1939 to 13th April 1940 29
CHAPTER 4 45
Deportation of Class Enemies - Przemysl to Dobrynovka 45
    13th April – 14th August 1940 45
CHAPTER 5 59
    To Hell and Back - Tochka et alia 59
    14th August 1940 – 10th September 1941 59
CHAPTER 6 92
A Better Deal - Karakanda 92
    10th September 1941 – 1st February 1942 92
CHAPTER 7 101
To England by Land, Sea and Desert 101
    1st February – 25th September 1942 101

CHAPTER 8 119
The Family in London 119
   1942 - 1945 119
CHAPTER 9 146
Settling in Our Adopted Country 146
   1945 onwards 146
Photographs 160

iv

TIME TO REMEMBER, TIME TO FORGET

INTRODUCTION

This is the story of the Dembinski family, of the coat-of-arms Rawicz. The genealogical tree of the family began in 1279. Through many puer genitas generations, both the 20th progeny and the 20th century are reached. This story encompasses all the members of this family in this epoch, and in particular the period of the Second World War of 1939-1945 when the family was thrown to the wind in all directions. Specifically, the storytelling is about the deportation of the family from Poland to Russian Asia and their journey through the Middle East to South Africa and then to England.

The essence of this story is taken from three sources: firstly, from remembrances of my parents, secondly from my sister's 1939 diary entries (to which I was privy after her death) and thirdly from the many postcard messages written between 12 members of the extended family which give the *'mis en scene'* of the life they led during this time. It is through their words that pictures can be built up about the deprivations they had to endure, often in the hardest of conditions imaginable. The postcards travelled between 12 countries and five continents.

All the historical notes in this book are extracted from various sources. The research and compilation of this story of fact, not fiction, took some time. There are my sister's diary notations from 1st September till 31st December 1939; her writing was exceedingly difficult to read so it may come about that some facts have been missed. Then there is my Mother's account from 1st September 1939 to 1st April 1942, ending when leaving Russia for Persia (now Iran) via the Caspian Sea. She dictated this account to me in Polish in 1945. It was written in an old exercise book and it stayed like that for many years. In 1987 I decided to translate it and my daughter, Anna, typed it up and put it in a folder. I called it 'Escape', a title which had relevance to a story I wrote while at St Louis Preparatory School in 1947, earning me 'a literary prize' at age 13. When I subsequently had access to my sister Tota's account of the first four months and compared it with my mother's account, I found a lot of discrepancies. I have used the information largely from Tota's diary.

Also included are excerpts from significant inter-communication between 22 members of the extended family. By 'extended' I mean not only the relationships but also the distances between 12 countries during the period of 1939 to 1945. These written records have been kept and contain very important information. We must remember that in those days even the telephone was not much in use and would have been difficult, as well as expensive, between correspondents in Poland, especially as 'the enemy had ears'. To telephone abroad would not have been possible – how useful it would have been to have had a mobile or smart phone! There were telegrams of course but again they were used very seldom and the cost would have been exorbitant at that time. So the written word was on postcards. These are interesting in their own right; those written in Poland (and that's 95%) have interesting stamps for the philatelist.

To begin with, German Hindenburg stamps were used and cancelled in Polish (Warszawa) or German (Warschau). It isn't until April 1940 that we see the first Polish stamp with the currency overprinted in German with the eagle and swastika. Finally around this time they issued stamps of the General Gouvernement, including the Hitler heads. The first card in my possession with the new Polish 'Poczta Polska' stamps of the Communist regime and still censored was dated 3rd October 1945. There are also cards sent by my Mother from Przemysl in the Russian zone from the early 1940s. All have Russian stamps and are cancelled in Russian.

As all mail was censored, writing postcards made it easier for the Censor to read. How they deciphered the Polish writing is beyond me but at least they didn't have to open an envelope to read the messages. There are examples of slashes across the envelope or card indicating that a German censor was using a chemical mark to determine that no invisible ink had been used in the correspondence.

I have used extracts from "Rising '44, The Battle for Warsaw" by Norman Davies, "Keeping the Faith – the Polish Community in Britain" by Tim Smith and Michelle Winslow, as well as several other books dealing with this part of the war history.

When war broke out in September 1939, I was five years old; my recollections are hazy and much is lost in the mists of time. The account given is true factually and historically. In this time frame I have interrupted the sequence of events by including interesting historical facts in regard both to the family members and to Poland's past.

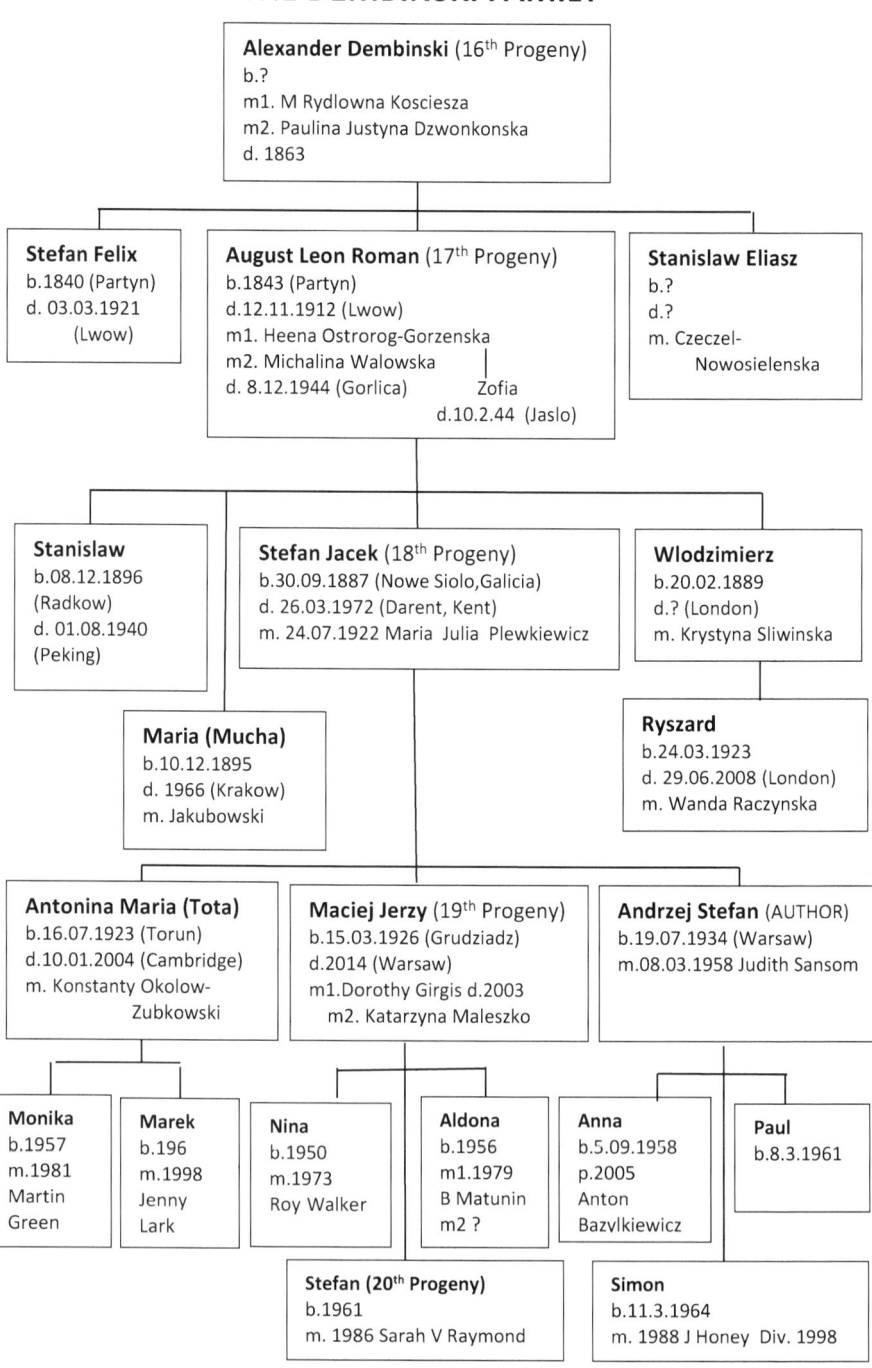

THE PLEWKIEWICZ FAMILY

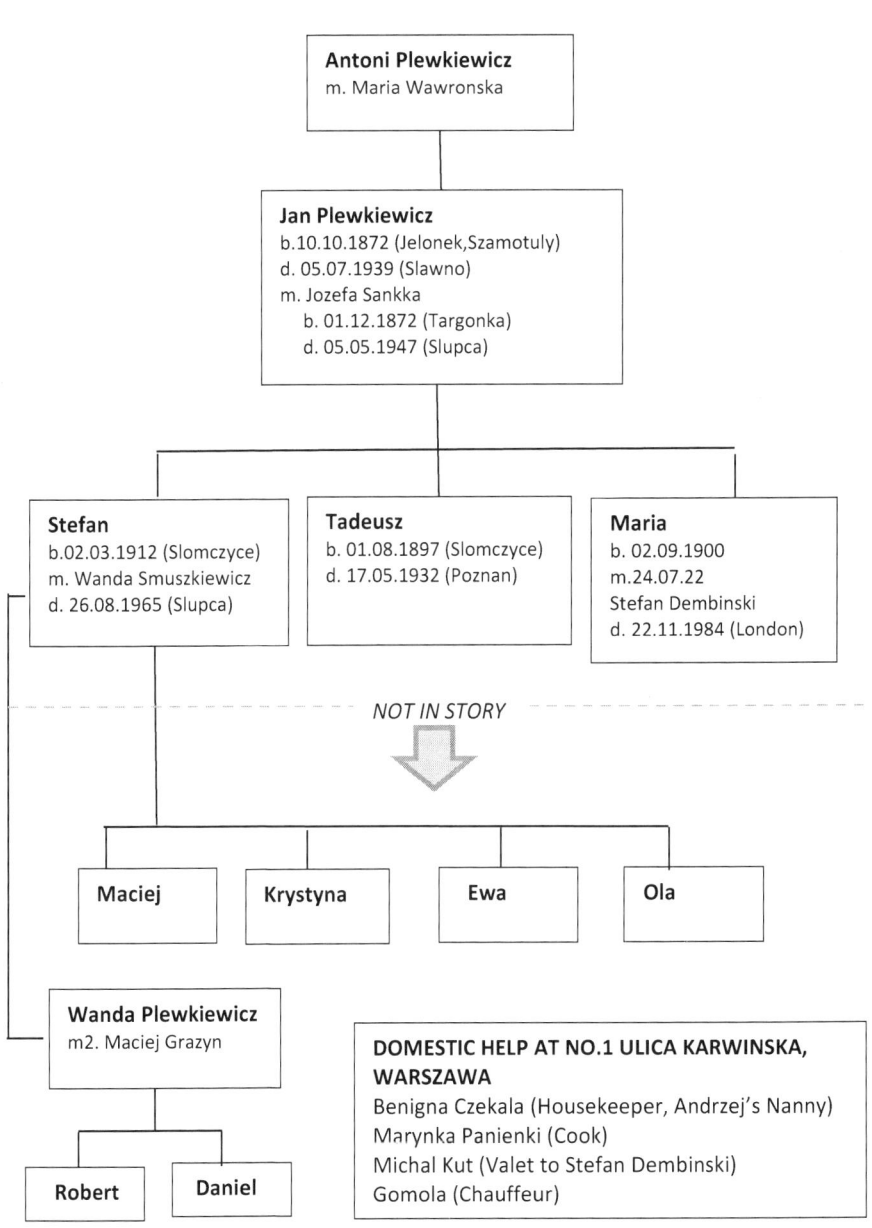

The Family Members in this Story

Age at 1.9.39		Relation to Author	Year of Death	Age at Death
-	Alexander Dembinski	Great Grandfather	1863	?
-	(Son) Stefan Felix Dembinski		1921	81
-	(Son) Stanislaw Elias Dembinski		?	?
-	**(Son) August Leon Roman Dembinski**	Grandfather	1912	69
c65	(Wife) Michalina Karolina Dembinska	Grandmother	1944	?
43	(Son) Stanislaw Dembinski	Uncle	1940	44
44	(Daughter) Maria Jakubowska	Aunt	1966	71
c65	(Daughter) Zosia Dembinska	Aunt	1944	?
52	**(Son) Stefan Jacek Dembinski**	Father	1972	85
39	(Wife) Maria Julia Alicia Dembinska	Mother	1984	84
13	(Son) Maciej Jerzy Jozef Dembinski	Brother	2014	88
5	(Son) Andrzej Stefan Jan Maria Dembinski	Author	2019	85
16	(Daughter) Antonina Maria Elzbieta Dembinska	Sister	2004	81
50	**Wlodzimierz Dembinski**	Uncle	?	?
37	(Wife) Krystyna Dembinska	Aunt	?	?
16	(Son) Ryszard Dembinski	Cousin	2008	85
-	**Jan Plewkiewicz**	Grandfather	1939	67
67	(Wife) Jozefa Plewkiewicz	Grandmother	1947	75
27	(Son) Stefan Plewkiewicz	Uncle	1965	53
-	(Son) Tadeusz Plewkiewicz	Uncle	1932	35
?	(Housekeeper) Benigna Czekala	N/A	?	?
?	(Cook) Marynka Panienki	N/A	?	?
?	(Valet) Michal Kut	N/A	?	?
?	(Chauffeur) Gomola	N/A	?	?

CHAPTER 1

PRELUDE TO WAR

My memories of this time are sketchy to say the least; being a child of five in 1939, I only remember snippets, incidents rather than a complete picture. However, by visiting the places, talking to relatives and, above all, researching the past, it is relatively easy to visualise most of that picture. What history! Some of it was cruel, some frightening, but also with some happy endings.

What did we leave behind in Poland? The family were owners of property, either belonging at this time to the Dembinski's or the Plewkiewicz's. In the province of Poznan on the Western side of Poland and near Germany there were two estates. This area was in Prussia up to World War I, 1914-18, and then from August 1919 was in Poland. From September 1939 it was occupied by Germany until its surrender in 1945. Poland was then ruled by the Communists until 1989 when it became part of Free Poland. People who lived here spoke Polish and German in a similar way that the French in Alsace speak two languages.

There was Slomczyce in the province of Konin with its village of Slupca. The estate had 321 hectares of land. Before the war it was managed by Stefan Plewkiewicz, Jan's son, who was born here in 1912. From all accounts he was not very successful. The estate was, of course, taken over by the Germans and he then worked in the town of Slupca during the war as a researcher in the accounts department.

From a card written in 1946, we learn that the estate was not subsequently taken over by the Communists. It is not until my sister's correspondence in the 1990s (when she tried to get the estate returned to us) that we learnt it had been taken over by the Agricultural Management division of the Polish Government, probably in the early 1990s. I have no recollection of ever seeing this holding, either before the war or in more recent times. As far as I know, it was quite near Slawno.

I vaguely remember Slawno. Jan Plewkiewicz (my Grandfather) with his wife Jozefa, owned both Slawno and Slomczyce. My memory of my grandfather is of an old man seated in his carriage with a big cigar in his mouth and being driven by his coachman around the estate with me on his knee, aged four. Is it possible that I can still smell that cigar, even now?

This estate of Slawno is in the province of Pila with its larger village nearby of Lubasz. I was christened on 27 August 1934 in the Church there; our parents got married there and our grandfather is buried in its cemetery – a large burial stone marks the spot. The estate comprised land measuring 1800 hectares (4448 acres), including the adjacent farms of Kamionka and Zmyslowa, as well as 890 hectares of forest. There is a lovely photograph (p160) from the old times of the 1930s showing a winter scene with a sleigh and four horses, a coachman in his furs waiting outside the front of the house.

It was here that my father, Stefan Jacek Dembinski, was married to my mother, Maria Julia Alicja Plewiciewicz, on 25th July 1922. There is a wedding photograph (p160), with each person identified by a number written on each face. There were 34 people in all, dressed in their fineries of that era. Amongst them and beside the groom and bride, are some of our relatives, about whom we will hear later on: Jan and Jozefa Plewkiewicz (grandparents), Tadeusz Plewkiewicz (uncle, who died 10 years later at the age of 35 and is therefore unknown to me), Michalina Dembinska (grandmother), Wlodzimierz and Krystyna Dembinski (uncle and aunt), Maria Jakubowska (nee Dembinska – aunt Mucha).

My grandfather, Jan, died in July 1939 at the age of 67 in Slawno. This was only two months before the war. One could say that he was lucky not to have to go through the horror of the German occupation. The house at Slawno was soon occupied by German officers in September 1939 and so Jan's widow, Jozefa, went to our house in

Warszawa and lived there, together with the servants, throughout the war.

On 22nd June 2009 my brother Maciej and I went to visit Slawno (photo p161). This was the second time that Maciej had returned here; the first time was in the 1990s together with our sister Antonina, known to all as Tota. For me especially it brought back 'wishful thinking'. Yes we would and should have inherited this magnificent estate.

By this second visit, Tota had died and, with Maciej resident in Canada and myself a citizen of the United Kingdom, neither of us would have been able to live on the estate. Anyway, it was already in other hands and we were shown around by the manager of the Agricultural Cooperative which had bought the estate from the Polish Government in the 1990s.

Approaching the property from the road through monumental gates, you arrive at the house via a sweeping drive. At the front of the house, wide balustraded steps ascend to a covered portico and there are six large windows upstairs, probably the bedrooms. At the back of the house there are more wide steps leading up from a lawn and eight large windows.

Entering the house, the rooms have very high ceilings and beautifully crafted wooden doors. When we saw these rooms, we were told by the manager that this Cooperative spent its own money in all the rebuilding and decoration of the rooms - and they had indeed done a wonderful job of the restoration – as good as a presidential palace. That is what it is – a palace; in fact I have seen some Polish tourist literature with Slawno Palace as the description. In England it would have been called a Manor House.

The bedrooms where the servants were housed had as yet not been touched and we were not shown the rooms. Underneath the house, there were of course cellars which would have been used for storage and perhaps the kitchen.

The manager then took us to visit the farm buildings, which were within a quarter of a mile of the house. Maciej remembered how they used to be before the war and what they were used for. There were many stables, buildings for carriages, grain stores and many other farm buildings. There was the vodka distillery with its high chimney and a carp pond which was more like a lake. It must have been very impressive when we lived there but that day it looked old and neglected.

At the back of the house was a large lawn and immediately beyond this were extensive woods which contained some magnificent trees, but of course, as it had not been maintained, it was now rather wild.

We were told that when the Russians went through on their way to Berlin in 1945, they took over the 'palace' and treated it rather like the Russian mud huts they were used to living in. They smashed the furniture, doors and windows, making fires on the parquet floors and stealing all the valuables – pictures, ornaments and anything else they could carry.

Our house in Warszawa was at No 1 Ulica Karwinska, Fort Mokotow XII (see p162). It was a modern house by the city's standards, newly constructed, with an area of 836 sq metres, and occupied by us on 25th May 1936. The district of Fort Mokotow is some distance from the city centre; in fact we lived here until 5th September 1939 and there were still fields and farmland at the back of the house. I remember we had a hunting dog called Jacques. It strayed onto the farmland one day and the farmer shot him.

I remember visiting this house with my elder brother Maciej. As I was only five years old when we left during the war, Maciej told me his memories of the house:

"That room was Ojciec's (Father's), next door was Matka's (Mother's), I shared a room with you Andrzej and Tota had the fourth room. I remember two reception rooms downstairs, one with large glass doors. They were large rooms with beautiful furniture, parquet floors and impressive lighting. I rather think one was the sitting room (salonik), the other the dining room. I have no recollection of the rest of the

house, but most probably there were at least three or four other rooms. The basement was used for the kitchen and servants' rooms."

Outside there was quite a large garden and I remember I had a sandpit somewhere. A separate large garage was adjacent to the house and both the front and rear entrances had large wooden doors.

In 1993 the house was rented out by the Polish Government (who requisitioned it in our absence) to the Columbian Embassy but at the time when I saw it, in 2007, it was the Estonian Embassy. I have a note that it was taken over by Skarb Panstwa (Polish Treasury) on 26th October 1955. We therefore could not see the inside of the house, only stand outside by the perimeter fence.

Beside our family of five, we had several servants. There was Benigna Czekala (housekeeper and my nanny), Marynka Panienki (Cook), Michal Kut (Father's valet) and Gomola (Father's chauffeur). During the German occupation, the first three and my grandmother, Jozefa Plewkiewicz, lived together as best they could. Benigna did travel with us as far as Przemysl, returning after we left for the steppes of Kazakhstan in April 1940. Gomola was with my Father till he left for Hungary. I must mention here my dog, a dachshund, which I loved and called 'Toffee'. Much later, in 1947 in England, I was given another dog; this time it was a Scottish terrier and it was again called 'Toffee' Mark II!

A few words about Poland's history might be a good idea at this stage.

Until 1918 Poland was divided between Russia, Prussia and Austria. The collapse of these empires in World War I enabled Poland to regain its independence in 1918. It also regained some Russian land by battles raging over its borders and it wasn't until independence was threatened by the Russians that full independence was finally gained in 1920. The country's brief period of independence ended in 1939 with the German and Soviet invasions. So, Warszawa prior to 1920 was under Russian rule. From September 1939 it was under the yoke of the General Gouvernement of Nazi Germany which came to an end in 1945 when the Communists took over for 44 years. In

1989 the Poles had had enough of Communism and, after the Solidarity Uprising, it became a free Poland once again.

So the above is a précis of the period 1918 to 1989. We now need to know the history of the time just before Hitler invaded Poland.

On 31st March 1939 Chamberlain, the British Prime Minister, announced a guarantee to Poland against aggression by Germany called 'The Anglo-Polish Treaty of Mutual Assistance'. This was a couple of weeks after Hitler marched into Bohemia and Moravia in Czechoslovakia. At this stage Hitler allowed the Hungarians to annex Sub-Carpathian Ruthenia, thus achieving the common frontier with Poland. So it was that our Father, Brigadier General Stefan Dembinski, led his group into Hungary and internment on 18th September 1939.

Germany's foreign minister, Joachim von Ribbentrop, demanded from Poland the return of Danzig and an extra territorial 'corridor' across Polish Pomerania; Poland refused. On 23 June 1939 Adolf Hitler gave the order to his General Staff to implement the preparatory plans of the war operation coded "Fall-Weiss" which he had made on 24 November 1938. The date for the attack on Poland was even then set for 1st September 1939.

Thirteen days before, on 10 August 1939, an 'incident' coded 'Operation Himmler' was arranged by the Nazis to give Hitler a reason to implement his war plans. A group of German SS men dressed in Polish uniforms, led by the Gestapo high-rank officer, Alfred Naujocks, would seize the German radio station at Gleiwitz situated near the Polish border. A broadcast would be made in the Polish language proclaiming that it was the time for Poland to invade Germany. Twelve or thirteen prisoners from a concentration camp, wearing Polish uniforms, were given fatal injections and left strewn around the radio station building as the evidence that all the attackers were killed. After the incident, members of the Press and other persons were to be taken to the scene and report to the world at large this shameful 'atrocity' and the Polish infringement of the German territory.

On 23rd August 1939 Ribbentrop, Foreign Minister of Germany, and Molotov, the Russian counterpart, concluded a Non-Aggression Pact containing clauses about the partition of Poland and allowing Russia to take over Lithuania, Latvia, Estonia and Finland. Still on the same day, 23 August, the British Ambassador, Sir Neville Henderson, presented a diplomatic note to Hitler stating that both Great Britain and France would honour their obligations to Poland (made on 31 March 1939) if Hitler's armies invaded.

On Sunday 3rd September the British Prime Minister, Chamberlain, having lost all his attempts at appeasement, made his famous speech in the House of Commons declaring war on Germany. France would follow within a day.

CHAPTER 2

Travellers' Tale - Warszawa to Przemysl

1st September to 8th November 1939

In the early hours of Friday 1st September, the German Wehrmacht crossed the Polish border at four places. The Luftwaffe bombed Wilno, Grodno, Brest Litovsk, Lodz, Katowice, Gdynia, Krakow and Warszawa. On the same day about 80 tons of gold reserve belonging to the Polish Treasury was secretly put onto a special train in Warszawa. It arrived in Romania, being then a neutral country. Later some of it was taken to Turkey, then onward to Lebanon and hence to both France and West Africa. It finally arrived split into three parts in Britain, USA and Canada. After the war it was returned to Poland.

Just before 1st September, Hitler briefed his Generals at Obersalzburg in the following words,

"Genghis Khan had millions of women and men killed by his own will and with a gay heart. History sees him only as a great state builder. I have sent my Death's Head units to the East with the order to kill without mercy; men, women and children of the Polish race or language. Only in such a way will we win the Lebenstraum that we need. Who after all speaks today of the annihilation of the Armenians?

Warsaw, as the enemy capital, attracted the Wehrmacht's special fury. It was mercilessly attacked by shrieking Stuka dive-bombers from the dawn of the very first day. It was surrounded on all sides from the second week of the campaign. Inspired by the mayor, who had been appointed Civilian Commissioner, the citizens threw themselves into the defence, fighting the fires, supplying the defenders, tending the homeless and burying the dead. The mayor,

Stefan S, a former soldier in Pitsudski's Legions, was young, energetic, eloquent and widely respected. He made his name in the crisis of September 1939, rousing the populace in daily broadcasts to defend the city, denouncing Nazi barbarianism." [1]

* * * *

We now reach both Tota's diary entries and my Mother's account. On 2nd September Tota is already writing about the bombing of Warszawa:

"Sirens shrieking and the noise of the German Luftwaffe fighters and planes. The bombing is as yet not anywhere near Karwinska; everyone is very nervous and no-one knows what to do. At midday we hear on the radio that both Britain and France have declared war. It being a Sunday, everyone goes to Mass." This of course is not strange in Poland. Can you imagine people in Britain going to Church when the city is being bombed?

"On the 4th September, the morning is cold but warms up by the afternoon when Father arrives, staying only 1½ hours. During this time he tells us that the situation is very serious; we have to pack our clothes and possessions as quickly as possible. Slight panic takes hold of everyone. What to take with us? Where are we to go?"

I am crying my eyes out as I have been told I cannot take Toffee, the dachshund, with me. Maciej and Tota are arguing and Mother is in a flap. Benigna (the housekeeper and my nanny) comes to the rescue. Marynka, the cook, collects food to take with us. We honestly believe that we are leaving just for a week, well maybe a month. No-one could know that we would not see Karwinska again for more than 50 years.

Everyone is awake by 5am on the 5th September. Warszawa is being evacuated. An appeal is being made to the RAF to aid Poland by sending their fighter planes to attack the German bombers. (Poland had very few planes and those were all destroyed in the first day of

---

[1] 'Rising 44' by Norman Davies

war. Unfortunately for Poland, both Britain and France prevaricated and in the end, apart from sending three planes, nothing was ever done to mutually aid Poland).

Father arrived to take Mother, Tota, Maciej, myself and my nanny Benigna in his car, driven by his chauffeur Gomola. Quickly the luggage was loaded into the car. Money and some jewellery came too; part of the money was in dollars, that is gold coins. I have no idea how many of these American double Eagle coins there were, but they became a staple exchange right through our journeys across Russia. I still have one of these and it is worth a few hundred pounds now. We headed for Lochow, only 8 miles out of Warszawa. All the way we watched the German planes coming to and from Warszawa. At one time, one of them followed the car and was about to machine-gun us before we got into a wood. Here we stayed for about an hour before attempting to leave it.

As soon as we arrived in this little town, we were told by some officers that we had just missed a very heavy bombardment. They were expecting the Germans to return and advised us not to enter the town but to hide in a nearby wood. By this time it was evening and we had to find somewhere to stay for the night. Eventually we came across a forester's hut and asked the owner whether we could stay in one of the rooms for the night. It was cold, dirty and without light. Fortunately Marynka had prepared some food for us before leaving Karwinska. We all bedded down as best we could, including Father. Nobody slept very much. Already we missed our comfortable beds.

Gomola had driven back to collect more of our belongings and on the next day he arrived early in the morning with the rest of our luggage. Father drove with Gomola to the town of Lochow. There he managed to find two rooms for us at a forester's house just outside the town. We bought a couple of straw mattresses and so made ourselves a little more comfortable for the second night. This house was near to the main road. Everyone was fleeing East; hundreds of cars, hundreds of carts, laden with possessions, all trying to get away from the advancing Germans – anywhere as long as it was towards the East.

On the morning of 7th September we are told that all the families must be evacuated from Lochow. We don't want to be separated from Father. He is of course on duty and is driving round the various units, some of which have got completely separated, with the officers not knowing which way to go.

In the afternoon, Father thinks that the best way would be to go by horse and cart to Kornoszymce, about 190 miles. This was soon dismissed as impossible; it would take ages and would be very uncomfortable. By the evening we hear that all the families are leaving. Father says we have to go by train tomorrow. He has received orders to proceed to Dubno. That night we slept in our clothes so that we would be ready to depart very early in the morning.

At 4am Father departed with Gomola to join the army units. This was the last time we were to see Father until 3 years later when we finally met again in Britain on 25th September 1942.

Somewhat later we went to the station and boarded a military train. We were delighted to meet up with Aunt Krystyna (Krzysia), her mother Mrs Sliwinska, and her son Ryszard (Rys), and from now on we would travel together. We also met many friends of ours from Warszawa. Soon we realised that the train was going to Tarnopol so had to get off and wait for the right train.

On the 9th September, having travelled about nine hours in cramped conditions, we arrived in the middle of the night at Horohon. We managed to get a horse and cart and went to see the Sheriff to find accommodation. He told us to drive a further 5 miles out of town to a house on the road but when we got there we found there were no rooms available. We went back to the station at Horohon and waited there till morning. Our friend, Mr Wisloloh found us there and proceeded to find rooms for us at a forester's house. This would be temporary as the owner was not keen on us staying with him, but at least we had a roof over our heads.

Next day we slept till 9am as we were all very tired. As it was Sunday, we of course went to Mass. Our Aunt, her Mother and Son are in a nearby house. Talk about being dispersed…..every day in a different place. We wonder where we shall end up. Somehow we had to keep our spirits up. Meals – well, there were not many – we had to try and buy food in the nearest town or village and hope that we could use the kitchen wherever we were. Benigna was of course still with us and she was of great help, looking after us all the time.

On the 11th September we picked up information from people about the Germans overrunning more and more territory. Another panic sets in. We find we will have to move again. We decide to bury some of Mother's jewellery, silver and also my Polish lead soldiers (just the type of thing Germans would be infuriated about and for which you could be shot). All were put in a tin box, wooden planks were placed around it and it was all put in a deep hole. We did not return to Poland until the 1990s and, by then, nobody could remember where we had stashed this treasure!

On 12th September we arrived at Chloniow where we were met by Count Krasicki and taken to the estate administrator's house at an old farm. We were given two rooms by Mr and Mrs Goszkiewicz who were most pleasant and looked after us very well whilst we were there. We bought some cooking utensils and managed to look after ourselves.

On the 13th it was very hot, like a heat wave. We kept hearing gunfire getting nearer. Just as we had found a pleasant place to stay with kind people, we now expected to have to be on our way once again and very soon.

"By September 14th Wehrmacht armour and infantry had surrounded Warszawa and the Germans under a flag of truce delivered a demand to the Poles for unconditional surrender. But instead of giving up, the people of Warszawa began to fortify the city.

Men, women and children worked into the night, digging trenches in parks, playgrounds and vacant lots. Wealthy Varsovian aristocrats were chauffeured to defence sites where they toiled alongside office workers. Trolley cars were thrown across boulevards; barricades of cars and furniture were erected in narrow streets. In many cases they were stopping the tanks by civilians dashing boldly into the street to toss burning rags under vehicles and throw Molotov cocktails into the tanks. Warsaw radio helped to carry on the battle in its own way. Every 30 seconds it transmitted portions of the Chopin Polonaise to tell the world that the capital was still in Polish hands.

Angered by the unexpected setback, the German High Command decided to pound the stubborn citadel into submission. In round the clock raids, bombers knocked out flourmills, gasworks, power plants and reservoirs. They then sowed the residential areas with incendiaries One witness passing the scenes of carnage enumerated the horrors: 'Everywhere corpses, wounded humans, dead horses....and hastily dug graves'.

Finally food ran out and the famished Poles, as one man put it, 'cut off flesh as soon as a horse fell, leaving only skeletons'". [2]

Between the 12th September and 8th October, we stayed in Chloniow. At last we were reasonably comfortable. In these three weeks we kept packing and unpacking our suitcases. We wanted to go to Lwow (1945 onwards Lviv in Ukraine). We listened to the radio. Lwow was being bombed. We couldn't get any form of transport; there were few trains and they didn't operate to a timetable any more. Then there was another tragedy for us and for Poland.

On the 17th September, Count Krasicki came over with the ghastly news that he had heard on his radio; the Russians had crossed the border into Poland. On his suggestion, Mother went into the town and asked the authorities to confirm that the news was true, which they did. We could hardly believe it. We were now caught between the Germans and the Russians, the former still advancing from the west and the latter arriving from the east. We were now in the worst predicament. What do we do, which way to go?

---

[2] 'Rising 44' by Norman Davies

We decided to sit tight and wait and see what happened. We still thought that it would possibly be better to return to Warszawa but everyone we spoke to had different ideas about where would be best to go. Nobody knew what to do and the stress of it all produced more panic. Some said the trains were not functioning, others said they were. You couldn't believe anyone. It looked as if we were stuck there.

On the 20th September, at 6pm, we saw the first Russian soldiers on horseback galloping towards the house where we were staying. It appeared to be the first Russian patrol. They stopped at the house to ask questions from the farm labourers as some of them could speak Russian. We stayed indoors until they had left.

We heard that the Polish Government, including President Moscicki and the Commander-in-Chief, Marshall Rydz-Smigty, had crossed the frontier into Romania (then a neutral country) at Kuty and were all interned. General Sikorski was among them but managed to escape. Poland therefore ceased to have a Polish Government.

As all the villagers were Ukrainians, they were overjoyed to see the Russian soldiers and we were soon shown that we were now their enemies. We tried not to set foot outside the gates of the estate. One day the militia came to search our miserable belongings to see whether they could find anything useful to 'confiscate' or, in other words, steal. Another day they came for the same purpose. Poor Tota was on her own as the rest of us were in the town shopping. She said in her diary: 'my legs and lips trembled'. They were more thorough this time and came away with some of Krzysia's mementoes and Maciej's camera. Luckily they could not open the suitcases as the keys were with Mother.

On 27th September we heard that Warszawa had finally surrendered. Warsaw Radio replaced Chopin's Polonaise with his funeral march. The Resistance lasted nearly four weeks. We should compare this with the three weeks in which France had surrendered.

As the Government was interned in Romania, a new government had to be chosen which would in future look after Polish interests and would soon be called the Polish Government-in-Exile (in London).

Count Raczynski, the Polish Ambassador in Britain, his counterpart Lukasiewicz in Paris and one or two others met to appoint the two chief members of the government. Actually, on being asked to resign, President Moscicki nominated to succeed him a man who was not suitable to the two ambassadors. Lukasiewicz chose three possibles: Ignacy Paderewski, the famous pianist and composer, who was deemed to be too old and infirm at 79 – and in fact died two years later, August Zaleski, who had been Foreign Minister 1926-32 – and who would become the next President in Exile in 1947. Lastly Wladyslaw Raczkiewicz, who had also been Minister of the Interior between the wars. Raczkiewicz was chosen to be President and General Sikorski was to be the Prime Minister and Supreme Commander of Polish forces abroad.

Just an interesting note about General Wladyslaw Sikorski; he had been a Chief of Staff 1921-2, Prime Minister in 1922-23 and Minister of War 1923-24. He had then retired as he did not get on with Marshall Pilsudski who was the Head of State from 1918-1935. I know he dealt with Father when he was the Head of the Military Secretariat in London, and in fact my Father represented the President at Sikorski's funeral. It was a great tragedy when Sikorski, his daughter Mrs Lesnowska and many other important personages were killed in an aircraft accident while taking off from Gibraltar at 11pm on 4th July 1943. My Father used to collect interesting covers (envelopes) and stamps for me as by then I had become a stamp collector. Among them was an envelope from Gibraltar postmarked 5th July and addressed to the President. The letter was not in the envelope but I was sure it was the envelope with the message about Sikorski's death.

Next I will include a few notes about Wladyslaw Raczkiewicz, President of Poland-in-Exile. I remember him well from the 1940s. His residence was in Stanmore, North London. I have a photograph taken when we all went there; in it I am playing darts against a dartboard on a tree in the lovely park. There is also a photo of Father playing bridge there with the President. Often I used to visit Father in the President's town residence at 34 Belgrave Square. The President looked very distinguished in his dark suit. He gave me a book signed by him at Christmas 1942 – it says "To my young friend Andrzej Dembinski" and was titled 'Sportsman's Bag' with 17 magnificent plates of hunting scenes. Also received from him was a 5 piece penknife which I've used ever since. Raczkiewicz died in 1947 and was succeeded by August Zaleski who had previously been Foreign Minister 1926-32 and 1939-41. I regret to say that his position of President-in-Exile did not amount to much after 1947 as the British Government no longer accepted the London-based Polish Government-in-Exile and instead accepted the Communist Polish Government in Poland.

At this stage, let us leave Tota's and Mother's narratives and give here a summary of what Father accomplished in the September 1939 campaign. It was written by one of the soldiers in General Dembinski's Group and I later translated it from Polish.

"10th September 1939 – The General is appointed to organise resistance around Sambor and Stryj, as well as the region from Dniester to the (new) frontier with Hungary. All was rather chaotic with units falling back before the Germans who were rapidly advancing. He was given to understand that he must lead by giving advice and hope and to be in constant contact with the commanders of different units. These were spread over huge distances and there were many difficulties. The units consisted of older soldiers, and these soldiers did not know each other. There was a lack of equipment and of transport. He managed to organise these odd units into a fighting force against the enemy. It is the most difficult thing to reorganise an army which is at the same time defending areas, then retreating, then defending etc. On 15th September the group now formed, consisting of three infantry regiments, secured Stryj and the villages in the forested region south-east of Stryj.

The group, commanded by Colonel Dudek, held onto Drohobycz. Their forward units were already in contact with the enemy near Sambor. Colonel Katowicz holds Turka.

The most heavily armed units were sent around the Dniester valley to protect Mikolajowa, Zydaczona and Zurawna.

The General also had to organise the Corps defending Pograwicz as well as some units of police.

Orders were given in regard to air attacks and to build obstacles on roads and on outskirts of villages against the German armoured division. They were told to fill as many bottles as they could find with gasoline.

15-16th September – Battles raged around Sambor continuously. Air bombardment around Stryj. A defence was organised in the vicinity of villages and forests. The various units knitted together much better now and there was more confidence.

16th September – Several high ranking officers arrived from the Headquarters and from the Carpathian Army. One of them is General Dabkowski, Commander of the sappers.

17th September – General Fabryca arrives. An idea is born to create a defensive enclave in the south-west region abutting onto Romania. At 12.30 that day, a message is received by telephone from the Army HQ that the Russian units have crossed over the Polish border. The order is given to avoid the Russians but keep fighting against the Germans. In the evening, orders are received from the Commander in Chief that General Dembinski is to march towards the Hungarian border.

18th September – General Dembinski's group leaves for the Hungarian border, passing through Dolina and Skola. The Germans are pressing hard near Sambor; in the morning they take Drohobycz and in the afternoon they get to Stryj.

The war in Poland is coming to an end. There are only a few still fighting in the region around Warszawa. General Dembinski's group, *marching towards the border, is getting sparser with many of the soldiers deciding not to leave Poland. Only those who want to continue to fight in the war, but outside of Poland, are now left.*

Before crossing the frontier in the region of Klimco, General Dembinski orders all the units to march past before the Polish Flag. When the soldiers look at the General he gives the command: 'Don't look at me, look at the Polish Flag while you are still marching on Polish soil. Soldiers cried. Many fell down to kiss the Polish soil."

Father took a pouch and filled it with Polish soil. He had it till his dying hours. His ambition was always to return to Poland taking the soil back with him. Unfortunately he could never achieve this ambition during the Communist Regime. He died in London on 26th March 1972 and is buried at Ealing Cemetery. Poland was finally freed from its Soviet yoke in 1989.

I will now relate some interesting historical facts about Poland's frontiers in September 1939; with Germany 1912 km, with Russia 1412 km, with Czechoslovakia 984km, with Lithuania 507 km, with Romania 349 km, with Latvia 109 km, with the Free City of Gdansk 121 kms, with the sea 140km, with Hungary unidentified. The distance between south and north was 903 km, between east and west 864 km. The population in 1939 was 34.5 million – 27.2% lived in towns and 72.8% in the country. The religions in 1939 were 64.8% Roman Catholic, 11.8% Orthodox, 10.5% Greek Orthodox, 9.8% Jewish, 2.6% Protestant, 0.3% others. All these facts would change dramatically by the end of the war in 1945.

A poet's version of the last days of Warszawa:

"And he, when the city was just a raw, red mass,
Said 'I do not surrender' Let the houses burn!
Let my proud achievements be bombed into dust.
So what if a graveyard grows from my dreams?
For you, who may come here, someday recall
That some things are dearer that the finest city wall"

The lost city was to be recalled with deep affection:

"Oh dearest Warsaw of my youth,
Which encompassed the whole of my world!
If only for a moment and in the dark
I wish to catch a glimpse
Of the ashes and the flowers
Of that good past!"[3]

Back now to Tota's and Mother's interpretation of events:

On 27th September we heard a Polish news bulletin from London that Warszawa was to surrender. The last fighting ended in the wilderness of marshland on 6th October, somewhere beyond the River Bug.

On the 28th September we heard about the signing of the German-Soviet Treaty of Friendship, Demarcation and Co-operation. In other words, how to carve up and decimate the culture and religion of Poland. This friendship did not last very long!

On the 1st October we were still in Horoniow. Some of the families who travelled with us decided to go on to Lwow. We heard that Lublin had been taken by the Russians. We still had this idea of returning to Warszawa but it was a forlorn hope. To travel through both the Russian and German armies would be impossible; neither would give us passes. We heard on the radio from London that the Germans had taken the Polish units who surrendered in Warszawa as prisoners-of-war. We wondered where they would end up.

We were told of the Russian rhetoric; as their tanks rolled into the towns and villages, they announced to the bewildered inhabitants that they had come to save them from the fascists. Molotov soon got on his pedestal to declare that Poland ceased to exist.

---
[3] Taken from 'Rising '44' by Norman Davies

On the 5th October the Fuhrer took the salute of the victorious Eighth Army in Warszawa; the march past lasted two hours. From the 1st to 25th September 6,376 people, mainly Catholics, were shot. The western districts were annexed to the Reich and were immediately 'cleansed' of a vast number of 'undesirables'. The central part adjacent to the Soviet zone with the banks of the River Bug, was set up as a separate 'General Gouvernement' and subordinated to SS Control, run by Hitler forces' legal expert, Hans Frank, whose nickname was Gestapoland' or 'Frank Reich'. He governed from the Royal Castle in Krakow which then became the capital. Historically speaking, Krakow was actually Poland's capital from 1038 to 1596 when it was moved to Warszawa. It was in Krakow's Wawel Cathedral that successive kings of Poland were crowned and entombed. Under the Partition of Poland of 1772, Krakow came under Austrian rule until 1918.

On 5th October we were still in Horoniow but the situation was becoming serious. The Russians arrested Count Krasicki and his father-in-law. A decision was made that the sooner we got to Lwow the better but Lwow was soon in Russian hands. We heard on the broadcast from London that Britain had sent forty divisions to France. At 1pm we heard General Sikorski's speech from Paris. He said that he had 10,000 Polish soldiers of the 6th Division in France.

All day during the 6th October we had been trying to find a cart and horses. Finally we managed to get permission from the military authorities in the town to borrow one on the next day. We piled all our belongings onto the cart so that we would be ready to go the following day.

On the 8th October we finally arrived at the station in order to catch the midnight train. It was only 1½ hours late. It was so packed with people that there was no way we could get on. We even had help from two kind men who helped us by looking for a place and carrying some of our luggage. However, none of us could find anywhere to squeeze into. At the last moment, as the train was about to depart, we gave the guard a fat tip and piled into the guard's van together with our suitcases. Aunt Krzysia, her mother and son were with us and so was Benigna. We all settled down to sit on our suitcases. At least we were all together, but any idea of sleeping was out of the question.

The train arrived in Lwow at 8am. Having disembarked by 9am, we got a taxi to take us to our new apartment comprising of three rooms. We managed to find this by getting in touch with a Mr G. Completely exhausted, all of us collapsed onto the beds and fell fast asleep. Once refreshed, some of us went out to get food, while the others unpacked and lit the fire as it was now cold and rained most of the day.

Benigna did most of the cooking; Maciej and Ryszard went daily to wait in the bread queue. I apparently just got in the way and was shouted at. Mother went out to buy the food, together with Krzysia, her sister-in-law.

And so the days went on. It rained every day. Mother met quite a few friends from Warszawa. Everyone was trying to get back to their homes so the discussions were usually about the various ways that we could use to return.

On the 10th the militia came to look over the apartment. They wanted to requisition it but after a while decided it was not to their liking. Aunt Krzysia's family were staying nearby in another apartment.

On Friday 11th October we were told that we had to register with the Soviet Authorities. So now they knew who we were. Maciej and Ryszard had borrowed a radio. Now we could listen to all the news. Mother was visiting her friends all day. Maciej and Tota were really bored and missed not going to school. You had to queue for everything, often for two hours, just for bread, but that's the life we now led and we soon got used to it. Every day was getting colder.

On the 19th we all went to be inoculated against typhoid and paratyphoid for the first time. We were advised to repeat the inoculations another couple of times.

The Russians were telling everyone that they had to vote. The problem is that nobody actually knew what they were voting for. They said 'Even if you are on your bed dying, you still have to vote'.

In the next week we got daily titbits of good news which didn't come to fruition. People went round with the latest such as "I only heard this morning that they are going to open the frontier." This type of news spread like wildfire and soon everyone knew it would be tomorrow. They all went back to their houses to pack everything and then sat and waited……..and nothing happened.

The Russian militia came again to requisition our apartment. Somehow we managed to avert this disaster. Then we heard the latest; the Germans will definitely open the frontier, but not here. It would be in Przemysl. So we decided we had to try and go there. Perhaps something would come of it and we could return to No 1 Karwinska. Another week went by.

By the 7th November we had checked the train timetable, packed everything once again and were ready to go the next day.

CHAPTER 3

Przemysl – The Frontier that Never Opened

8th November 1939 to 13th April 1940

On 8th November we got up at 5am. At 6am we made a start. We put all our suitcases into a taxi and soon arrived at the station. Hoping that we had found the right train, we all got in, as usual packed like sardines. However, by talking to others we found that this train was not going to Przemysl. Panic! We all got out again; by all I mean the four of us plus Benigna and then Krzysia's family of three. At the last minute we found the right train. This time we had to climb through the windows into a compartment already full with people. Somehow the suitcases were handed in.

Thank goodness the journey was only two hours. As it was, we were nearly crushed to death. Having arrived in Przemysl, Mother left us in the train. Most of the passengers had now got off. She went to investigate when and where we could cross the frontiers and of course how to get a permit to do so. All Mother found was mile-long queues. After a long and fruitless search she returned to the train which, when she left it earlier on, was in a siding. On reaching the spot, she found the train had vanished; no trace of either the train or us! Had the train departed elsewhere to some unknown destination? There was nobody to ask. She ran desperately from one railway line to another, checking each train, each carriage. Finally, physically and emotionally exhausted and having nearly given up, she saw three carriages on their own, a long way from the station, in another siding. We were in the third carriage and waving wildly to her. The reunion was ecstatic, with Mother shedding many tears of joy.

We spent that night sitting or lying on benches in the station waiting room. The place was very dirty and unpleasant.

Very early in the morning of the 9th, Mother went to try and get permits again….without success. Later that day we found out that there was a slim chance of getting them if one was accompanied by a young child. So, at 5 years old and by no means a baby, I was bundled into a large shawl. Mother carried me to the office where they were giving the permits and went cheekily straight to the front of the queue. The disguise did the trick because the militia let her through. Mother obtained permits for all of us, including Benigna. While she was there she decided that she may as well try and get three more for Aunt Kryzsia, her mother and son Ryszard. Mother waited until a new girl came on duty and, using the same trick as before, she managed to obtain them. On returning, she was very proud of her achievement. We had to sleep in the waiting room again that night.

On the 10th November, we managed to rent two rooms which were reasonably comfortable but very cold. It was just outside the town centre so quite useful as it was near the border. It was owned by an old NCO (non-commissioned officer) and he charged us 50 Groszy per day.

Every morning at 5am we got up and walked to wait in the queue by the frontier crossing, and each day we were told 'Tomorrow, tomorrow', but tomorrow never seemed to come. We heard that soldiers were being let through so perhaps civilians as well. Each time we carried our suitcases with us to be told 'Come back tomorrow'. We thought that they were doing this on purpose and that we would never make the crossing.

The frontier was the River Bug between the territory occupied by the Russians and the one occupied by the Germans. Every day we waited with all the others from 5 till 9 in the cold mornings. Often it was raining. We had to be there just in case one day we would be let through. In our rooms we cooked our breakfast and supper, but for lunch we went to a local club or café where we could get two courses for two zloty per person.

On 14th November, we were told that we would soon be unable to cross the frontier for another month or two so of course we were most depressed. We knew we couldn't do anything except stay where we were. What was worse is that we were not allowed to write to anyone. Father was somewhere, but where? Some of our relatives already knew that Father was in Hungary. The first card from Maria Mucha Jakubowska (our aunt) to our Father was dated 2nd November: *"Up to now there is no news from Maria and the children, nor from (aunt) Krystyna. We are safe and well."* This was written from Warszawa.

However, somehow we managed to get news out to our grandmother, Jozefa Plewkiewicz, who was still living on the estate in Slawno. She then wrote on 17th November to Father in Hungary saying: *"Everything is alright with Maria and the children and soon will be coming back. The house is in order (Karwinska, Warszawa), Marynka and Michal are living there"*. I believe that she probably thought we were still in either Horoniow or Lwow. (See p170)

On the 18th November our luck did not last. We were asked to leave our rooms so we had to find other accommodation. Mother trudged up and down the streets, from house to house, looking for unoccupied rooms. As soon as the owners found out that there were three children, they did not want to know. In Mother's own words: *"Finally I found a house belonging to a warrant officer who was already giving a room to Krzysia and her family. The couple were very kind people, giving up one corner of their own room for us. We had to pay him 15 Zloty per night but at least we had a roof over our heads. The man brought for us bread from the co-op in which he worked. His wife let me cook in the kitchen. We only had one bed but we are getting used to this kind of living."*

On 19th November the Russians promised that the frontier crossing would be opened that day. So, once again, everything got packed and we dragged our suitcases with us down to the frontier. As always we waited patiently for hours in the queue. It required us to cross the railway line, then walk over the bridge over the River Bug to Lasiane, just the other side of Przemysl. We waited until after midday when one of their officials came to tell us that the border would not be opened that day. No comment was made from the official when asked when the opening would be. So back we came with all our suitcases, discouraged and disappointed for the umpteenth time.

On the 20th November Maciej and Tota bought some cards, put some Polish stamps on and asked that they be cancelled in Russian lettering. They obviously knew that they would be worth money sometime in the future. Later on, Maciej wrote to Father, *"Could you please buy for me Hungarian stamps. I have bought for you Russian stamps with Polish cancellations"* – in other words, the other way around.

We heard on the radio that the Germans would move out 900,000 Poles from Pomorze and Wielka Polska provinces, as this area had been annexed to Germany. They would bring in their own farmers and other tradespeople to take over the towns and countryside.

"The Gestapo established its control over Warsaw in the early months by filtering the entire population, allocating them to racial categories and issuing them with the relevant documents. In order to live, every person required a Certificate of Racial Origin, an identity card (Kennkarte) and a ration card. Identity cards and ration cards were issued in accordance with the recipients' racial classification. This classification was drawn up in a strict hierarchy of superior and inferior groups and with the clear intention of separating those whom the Nazis wanted to prosper from those who were doomed to fade away."

Racial Group			*Daily Ration in Calories (1941)*
	(Germans	Reichsdeutsch (Germans from the Reich)	2613
Aryans	(	Volksdeutsch (Ethnic Germans)	2613
	(Non Germans	Suitable for Germanisation	669
		Mischlings (mixed race)	669
		Non Germans unsuitable for Germanisation	)
Non Aryans		Jews defined by descent	) 184
Sub Humans		Homosexuals	)
		Gypsies, imbeciles, incurables	)

"Once this system was in place, Varsovians were entirely dependent on their wits and on possession of 'correct' documents. The SS and the Gestapo who controlled it were backed up by militarized German police, by the local 'blue police' and by a ubiquitous army of informers. Anyone could be stopped on the street, arrested on suspicion, or, as increasingly happened, shot on the spot." [4]

I now go back to extracts from Tota's diary below and family postcards:

"21st-30th November – The latest news around the town was that the Germans would never open the frontier so we might as well forget about any ideas about returning to Warsawa. However, although quite illogical, the human mind still dreamed that 'perhaps' 'possibly' 'maybe' they would change their minds.

The days had become warm, nights cold and there was rain on most days in the week. There were shortages of food; bread was now hard to come by, there was no sugar and when it somehow surfaced, it cost a fortune – 15 zloty per kilo. Soap was unobtainable."

---

[4] Rising '44 by Norman Davies

Maria Jakubowska's card, dated 27th November, from Warszawa to Stefan Dembinski (her brother) in Budapest, told him that we were all in Przemysl awaiting to cross the frontier. There is also a card, dated 3rd December, from Father (he calls himself G. Egry from Kelsolyo Ucca 2-A Budapest) to Stanislaw Dembinski c/o Polish Embassy, Shiba-Ku, 9 Mita Tsunamchi, Tokyo, Japan. It tells him that their mother Michalina had been found with Zosia in Jaslo. Also that Wlodzimierz (Father's brother) came to see him on his way *(*to France I believe*)*. "*My house was hit by shrapnel and gunfire (Karwinska) and of course got looted but it will be possible to return to it*". He said that Krzysia and Ryszard were with Marysia (Mother), Mother-in-law (Jozefa Plewkiewicz) was well. "*Mucha (Maria Jakubowska) has got her job. Mucha said that your books (Faust etc) were saved – it was lucky they were put into the cellar.*" This card tells of the anguish Father had over the last two months, not knowing anything about his wife's and children's whereabouts.

On the 4th January, Father received a letter from Stanislaw in Tokyo, posted on 4th December. Father then sent him a card on 9 January 1940 from Budapest to Tokyo telling him that Marysia, Krzysia, Mrs Sliwinska and all children are in Przemysl and waiting to cross the border.

On 8th February Mucha sent a card to Stanislaw in Tokyo. The card postmarked in Warszawa (still in Polish) with a sub-heading 'Via Siberia'. The stamp is a Hindenberg German stamp overprinted Deutsche Post. It says "*As I received your card dated 1st September 1939 three days ago* (ie over 4 months from date of sending from Japan)*, I will try to write. Perhaps mine will be also lucky* (to arrive) *and you will receive it in a few months' time. Every one of us has found himself in a different place, like seeds of corn being sown in the wind. I was very worried about you, your collection and manuscripts. I still do not know what has happened to them.*" There is one more letter from Mucha to Stanislaw posted on 15th August 1940 to Peking. Stanislaw had already died on 1st August 1940 in Peking.

Maciej wrote a card on 16th July 1940 from Suvaluvka in Russia to Stanislaw Dembinski c/o Mr Hope Johnstone, Peking, China. He says, *"I am writing to you from Asia. They brought us here in cattle trucks. The journey was very tiring. They gave us very little food and that was awful. We hope to return home. Polish towns were not badly damaged during the war – Lwow less badly, Warszawa more. Ryszard and I work on the land. It is 80 km to the nearest town but it is forbidden for us to go there anyway. There are 31 Poles in our village who all came with us. It is 50-60 degrees so very hot but the nights are very cold. Auntie Krysia has received some money from Lwow a couple of times."* (It is doubtful that Stanislaw would have received this letter before he died on 1st August).

I will now quote from my Father's memento of his brother Stanislaw:

"He was born on 8th December 1894 (so he was 7 years younger than Father) *at Radlon. He was the most intellectual of the three brothers but the weakest in health. He had scarlet fever as a child. In 1914 he joined the Polish Army, however after only a few weeks he was sent to a hospital and discharged because of his weak heart. He went to Vienna where he attended a course at the Academy of Fine Arts. He tried amateur drama, studied banking – changing from one to another depending on his fancy at that moment. In 1920 he joined the Polish Army again – this time as a volunteer to fight against the Bolsheviks. Once again he landed up in hospital and had to give up.*

After the 1914-20 War, Stanislaw moved to Warszawa, but it was not long before he departed to Paris and then to Algiers. In Algiers he met and married a Polish artist like himself. He soon left her and Algiers and returned to Poland. He then worked in banking, moving to a commissariat in Gdansk. At this time he was translating old Greek poetry and works of Goethe into Polish, including Faust. These translations were in beautifully written Polish verse and often beautifully illustrated by calligraphy in Gothic writing with each initial letter on each page standing out. His work on Goethe was sent to Germany for the Goethe Exhibition. Unfortunately it was never printed as the cost of it would have been prohibitive.

Stanislaw was always interested in the Far East. Among many languages he could speak and write in Japanese and Mandarin. He spent much time in the Polish Embassy in Tokyo and later went to Peking, also in a position at the Polish Embassy. He died there on 1st August 1940."

Incidentally, I don't think anyone in the family – in England at least – knew anything of what happened to all his manuscripts. Stanislaw collected much Japanese art. On his death or perhaps, as I believe more likely, in the 1960s, the whole collection was sent to my brother, Maciej, in Montreal, Canada. In 2002 he decided to donate it to the National Museum in Warszawa. In making this donation, he met Katarzyna Maleczko, who was one of the directors specialising in Japanese Art at the Museum. They continued to see each other, started a relationship and were married in 2011.

There was another donation in 1971, or so it says in a Museum note. This time it is from Father. During the war years, he bought many lithographs while in London. I can still remember him in the 1940s and 1950s sitting at his desk in his bedroom in Clapham, studying and indexing with a magnifying glass. His collection contained 2000+ engravings and albums. Included in the masterpieces were engravings by Lucas van Leyden, Cornelis Cort, Carracci, Hollar, Bartolozzi, Earlom and graphics by the Rubens school. The themes depicted were of the animal kingdom, mythology, landscapes, and a few portraits. It covered the 16th to 19th centuries of European Engravings, with a special mention of an English mezzotint from the 18th century. He actually donated this in 1957. It would be worth a fortune now.

So now let me finish with Tota's diary entries between 1st and 31st December. At the same time we can see what information we can glean from the relatives' postcards.

In the first week of December, I was apparently laid up with measles. The weather was reasonably warm and we were thinking we would be spending Christmas here in Przemysl.

On 27th December Maria Jakubrowska was writing a card from Bagatela 14/28, Warszawa, to her brother (my Father) in Budapest saying that she had heard from Jozefa Plewkiewicz in Slawno that she had received a telegram from Marysia Dembinska from Przemysl saying that she was waiting for the frontier to be opened. Maria says that she is writing this to her brother as the first news of our whereabouts. She says that Gomola came to see her over Christmas and she is trying to get him some work with the prospect of a 50:50 chance.

In Przemysl we have the first day of frost; the first of many. The winter of 1939/40 would be remembered as one of constant freezing weather and much snow and it would continue up to the middle of March.

Money was running out. We started selling our belongings. We managed to get 1040 zloty for grandfather's silver watch. Once again we heard that we would be allowed to go over the frontier; first we were told it would be on the 19th, then the beginning of the New Year. We were packing and unpacking all the time. We tried to believe what they said. By now we should have learnt to disbelieve, to realise it was a pack of lies but the human in you wants to believe the 'good' rather than the 'bad'. So tomorrow, tomorrow never comes.

The Russians had taken the Polish zloty out of circulation and therefore it was worthless. Then the next day they revoked the order and advised that it was still allowed to use the Polish money. Typical, the Russian administration had no idea what they were doing.

On Christmas Eve we went for the umpteenth time to the frontier, but it appeared that only Germans were allowed to cross and they were only permitted to take 25½Kg of belongings with them on the train. We returned and had a very unhappy 'Wigilia' (Christmas Eve).

From a postcard to Father, Jozefa Plewkiewicz tells him that she has now moved from Slawno to Karwinska in Warszawa. She arrived there on 15th December 1949.

On the 25th, Christmas Day, the Germans put up a Christmas tree on the opposite side of the River Bug – it didn't make us any happier with them.

On the 26th we heard that a train had pulled in at Premysl station, full of wounded Polish soldiers, and that General Anders was among them. Mother went to see him and ask him if he knew what had happened to Father but he had no information about his whereabouts. A couple of times Mother went to take shoes and clothes for the wounded men. The following day the train had gone. How many of those wounded soldiers would be seen again? General Anders we would meet again in early 1942 on our way out of Russia.

The winter had really got into its stride; -11°C on one day, -22°C another day. Maciej had a fever. We were all very cold.

On the last day of 1939 we went out to sell Father's fountain pen for 30 Zloty. Gold was now 53 Zloty per gram. We sold 16.5 grams. No-one was celebrating the New Year – it couldn't be worse – or so we thought at that time!

There was a series of at least 12 postcards written between February and April 1940 from Mother in Przemysl to Father in Budapest. The first one was written on 3 February when she wrote that it was only today that they were allowed to send postcards, that she had received two telegrams from him and also received a postcard from Warszawa from Jozefa Plewkiewicz (her mother) which took one month to arrive.

She received the first postcard from Father on 7th February, written on 8th January, so the post, not only between the Germanised part of Poland to the Soviet occupied zone but also from a neutral country, ie Hungary, was very slow but usually got there. Relatives writing to Father addressed him as G Egry and when he signed himself, it was by the alias of Antoni Maciejewicz; this was all due to the need to keep his name and situation a secret.

On the 4th February Mother wrote that the weather was freezing, that we had enough to eat and were living primitively. Mother had a bed which she shared with me while Tota and Maciej were on straw mattresses on the floor. Benigna was still with us.

Three days later Mother wrote that "*Andrzej has a fur coat made from rabbit skins*". Also she said that we were running out of clothes – all we had fitted into three suitcases and three haversacks.

On the 12th February, on another card, is the following passage to Father. "*The longer I stay here, the more I long for you. I don't know what to do for the best. I have never been in a position where I had to face such problems on my own before. I feel very sad and lonely. What future is there for us? Why can't we be together? Lots of snow and freezing weather without a break since December.*"

On the next day she writes to Father: "*We are still here waiting to go home, but not to Warszawa. We will most probably go to 'the fatherland of Gregory' (*by which she means Russia*). It is a very long way from here so I am not keen on this to say the least. The children are not worrying, why I don't know. It is a sorry state of affairs. If only God could point us in the right direction, otherwise I don't know when we shall see each other again.*" (see p169).

On the next day she writes again about going to the 'fatherland of Gregory'. This is interesting and reveals that somehow Mother knew that we would be sent into Russia more than two months before the long journey actually took place. Both Tota and Maciej, reading these cards 50 years later, were truly astonished.

During the rest of February Mother writes to Father in Budapest, mostly complaining again about not receiving any news from him, of still having hope that the Germans would let us go over the frontier and get back to Warszawa, but this hope receded as time went on. She complains about the severe weather, of 30 degree frost, of chilblains, of time hanging heavily on our hands.

She said she got very depressed at times – *"to be left alone, I was so afraid. I never thought we would have to go through these times."*

On the 12th February, Maciej wrote a postcard to Father: *"We are all well. Could you please buy for me Hungarian stamps. I have bought for you Russian stamps with Polish cancellations. There are more stamps in Lwow – altogether they cost 16 roubles. For the last couple of days we had 20° of frost. It snows all the time. Mother is learning Russian and Tota learns German. Normally we are bored and we read books around the paraffin heater."* On the same card Tota says: *"I don't know what to do about our schooling as we will be losing a whole year. It's not possible to get a private tutor as we have not the money to pay for one."*

Even by the 15th March the Russians were still promising the border would be opened but nothing happened.

The last card from Przemysl, from Mother to Father in Budapest, says: *"On returning from Church on Sunday, the 31st March, Andrzej was leaning out of the window and shouted that there was a postcard from you and also one from my mother in Warszawa. It appears that the house (Karwinska) is not badly damaged and the window panes have been mended. Marynka broke her leg. I don't know about Stefan (Plewkiewicz, her brother) – probably he is still in Slupca. Unfortunately we are still here. What irony. In Warszawa a big empty house and here we don't even have our own rooms."*

At this stage, let me bring Father's journal up to date. I left him crossing over the frontier into Hungary on 18th September 1939 with the remainder of his Army Group.

As soon as he crossed over the frontier, he and his soldiers were interned. They laid down their arms and equipment. They were then directed to special transit camps, the largest of which was located at Raho and Losoncs. From the transit camps, the Poles were soon sent to places of internment under the instruction of the Hungarian General Staff. There were 88 camps, 6 hospitals and one sanatorium.

Father was made Head of Mission of the Polish Army Representation in the Kingdom of Hungary. His actual title was Representative of the Polish Army Interned in the Kingdom of Hungary. Matters relating to allocation and inventory of Polish military equipment were placed under orders of the III (Equipment) Group of the Ministry of Honveds. The Hungarian General staff had authority in general matters relating to internment, especially in the territorial allocation of internment camps. Surveillance and counter-intelligence in the camps were conducted by the II department of the General staff. This department was engaged especially in hunting down internees attempting to escape to the Polish Army in France. Father was based in Budapest and from there he organised the camps. His address was firstly at the Polish Legation at Orszashaz Ucca 13, then Kekgolyo Ucca 2A when postcards were addressed as G Egry, and later to Tukor Ucca 2. There is correspondence to him not only from his wife from Przemysl but also from Maria Jakubowska (sister) and Jozefa Plewkiewicz (mother-in-law) both from Warszawa; from Michalina Dembinska (mother) from Jaslo and from Stanislaw Dembinski (brother) from Tokyo, Japan.

After seven months of internment, he and a couple of officers managed secretly to evade being stopped in a car, driving through Switzerland and into France, arriving there in April 1940. In Paris he became in charge of the Polish cavalry department. This did not last for very long as France was being quickly overrun by the Germans. He evacuated to England, together with all the Polish Government and the Polish Army, arriving in England on 26th June 1940 (as per Father's British Registration Certificate). He was sent to Scotland where he commanded two of the camps, one of which was on Rothesay (see p164).

At this stage I will try to piece together information about another two members of the family, neither of whom I remember personally.

One was Zofia (Zosia) Dembinska. It took me a long time to find the relationship. Father's Father (my grandfather), August Leon Roman, married twice. The first marriage was to Helena Ostrorog-Gorzenska, granddaughter of General Turno, heir to a large estate near Wlodzimierz Wolicki. She died giving birth to a daughter, Zofia. Father says in his memoirs that Zofia had smallpox as a child. She became a teacher and worked all her life in Jaslo, near Tarnow, approximately 50 miles east of Krakow and therefore near the Carpathian mountains. She lived at Mostova 12 together with our grandmother Michalina Dembinska, nee Wolonska. Michalina was August's second wife. My Father remembers her as follows:

"At the beginning of the First World War, she had to leave Lwow and went to Vienna. At the end of the war, by which time she was a widow, she could not return to her house in Lwow as everything in it had been plundered. Instead she settled in Krynica earning a living by having a boarding house."

Krynica was then and is now a health resort, fashionable and luxurious. It had a sanatorium, only completed in 1939. The town is surrounded by the tree-covered Carpathian mountains which reach a height of 8,700 ft and in winter it is a ski resort. Remote areas of the mountains are inhabited by lynxes, wolves and bears.

Michalina Dembinska writing to Stanislaw Dembinski in Tokyo from Krynica on 18th December 1938 says the temperature was *"-20°... they are forecasting a very hard winter".* It seems that the winter of 1938/39 was just as cold as 1939/40.

My Father continues describing her:

"My family and I used to go and stay with her during the summer holidays (I wonder whether I stayed there?). *During the German occupation she went to live with her stepdaughter Zofia. Her own daughter Maria or Mucha Jakubowska nursed her on and off over the last year. She suffered from sclerosis and a weak heart. She was turned out of the rented house and had to travel in a horse and curt to Gorlice, where her daughter found a railway men's house as she was very ill. She died there on 8th December 1944. She was buried in the cemetery at Gorlice."*

I may as well include Maria Jakubowska. Everyone knew her as Aunt Mucha, literally translated as 'fly' but don't ask me why she was called thus. Father says this about his sister:

"She married A. Jakubowski, a Polish officer but he soon left her, going off to Vienna, and there he divorced her. During the war she lived at Bagatela 14/28 in Warszawa. Later she went to live in Krakow and lived at Bandurskiego 34, where she died in 1966."

Although the next correspondence may be out of chronological order, these three ladies - my grandmother, her step-daughter and my aunt – all played a role together and certainly with the rest of the family.

Stefan Dembinski (Father) hears first from Mucha on 9th February 1940. She gives the information that Marysia (diminutive of Maria, my mother) was believed to be in Krakow. On the same day Father was sent a postcard by Michalina in which she said that she was staying with Zosia (diminutive of Zofia) at Staszica 2, Jaslo with the same information about Mother and ourselves staying in Krakow. I don't know how they got hold of this information as we were never in Krakow. Also Mother was not allowed to send postcards (by the Russians) out of Przemysl until 3rd February. It is interesting to note that Father had written in pencil on both of the above cards the date he received them – 11th February – so taking only 2 days to arrive in the post from Poland under German occupation to Hungary! Michalina also says, *"It is quite quiet, we are well and not hungry."* Zosia appends a couple of lines asking about Staszek (diminutive of Stanislaw) and that she is very uneasy about him.

A couple of days later, Mucha wrote to Father, with the correct news this time, that Marysia (Mother), Krzysia (diminutive of Krystyna), Mrs Sliwinska and all the children were in Przemysl and waiting to cross the frontier. This must be the first time that Father had at last found out where we were. (Although I stated in the last paragraph that Mother could only send postcards from 3rd February, I now believe that she could communicate to Warszawa by card. It was only

43

forbidden to send cards abroad before 3rd February, ie to Hungary.) Mucha says, *"I am thinking how I can get them back here (to Warszawa). I thank God for his mercy on me – my belief is that we will all get together again, including our mother."* She was wrong on both counts.

On the 16th January, Michalina in Jaslo still thought we were in Krakow. She was very worried about the whereabouts of Wlodek (dim of Wlodzimierz) and that Zbyszek(dim of Zbigniew) was a POW and probably in Russia by now. I have not found out who this Zbyszek was in our family.

Michalina Dembinska wrote again on 18th January to Father in Hungary: *"Jesus Christ and Our Lady are looking after all of us. I am sure that in the end we will find each other again. It seems to me that we have all lived bad lives and we have to pay the price. People will never learn."*

Zosia Dembinska wrote to Father in Budapest on 3rd February: *"Winter is much harder than usual. We have a gas heater so we are better off than some."* Both Zosia and Michalina now knew that we were in Przemysl and not Krakow. She says, *"Mummy (ie Father's Mother) is determined not to fall ill."*

CHAPTER 4

DEPORTATION OF CLASS ENEMIES - PRZEMYSL TO DOBRYNOVKA

13TH APRIL – 14TH AUGUST 1940

"Stalin, in his wisdom and adhering to the Soviet ideology, wanted to ensure that Poland, or at least the part which they had overrun, was cleansed of all 'undesirables'. Hitler's idea of 'undesirables' meant primarily Jews and secondly anyone who was not 'Aryan'. The Soviets introduced a pseudo-social system where political and ethnic discrimination overruled all attempts at general class analysis and where Communist party membership opened the gates to the only master class. Everyone was declared a Soviet citizen. Russians and other East Slavs enjoyed preferential treatment, as did so-called 'workers and peasants'. Twenty one categories of 'enemies of the people', everything from gamekeepers to philatelists and including all 'bourgeois' politicians, all state employees, all private employers and all religious leaders, were targeted for elimination. In those early months of 1939-40, the Nazis shot 50,000 civilians in so-called reprisals, 15,000 political and religious leaders and 2,000 Jews. They also created ghettos for Jewish settlement in each of the main cities. They founded several concentration camps including Auschwitz for local political suspects, removing tens of thousands of innocent people, including priests, from circulation. The NKVD arrived with huge lists of names and addresses for immediate arrest. In that first winter they started the vast operation of deporting 1.8 million people either to the Arctic camps or to forced exile in Central Asia. Many would never return."[5]

---

[5] 'Rising '44' by Norman Davies

So what category of 'enemy of the people' did we come under? Military, political, professional, intellectual? Future representatives of Polish culture and education? Even philatelists? Yes, to a smaller or larger extent we could be classified under any of them but I still wonder on which list we actually appeared.

As mentioned previously, anyone living in the Soviet occupied areas in Poland had to register their names and who they were – which for women meant giving the name and occupation of their husband. Due to Father's officer status, we must have been on the military/intellectual/ aristocracy lists. Knowing Mother, and how proud she was of her name and standing, she would have registered the truth and only the truth in regard to Father's status.

And so what Mother thought would happen to us, did happen. In the middle of the night, 3am on Saturday 13th April 1940 (the unlucky 13th), we were woken up by the banging of doors and the shout of '*Odkrywaj Dwory!*' Opening the door, Mother found an official from the NKVD (Russian secret police) and behind him four soldiers who all entered the house at once. They strode into the room where we slept, shone a torch into our eyes and told us to dress. *"Get all your belongings together"* the official said. We were all in shock. What on earth was going on? At last, now fully awake, Mother asked what it all meant. Were they requisitioning this house? In the middle of the night? The only answer we received was that we were going to be moved further away from the frontier. That sounded ominous. None of us suspected how much 'further away' this would be.

We packed everything we had, not that there was very much of it. The official said *'take everything, you will need it.'* The soldiers helped us to carry our three suitcases and three haversacks, plus boxes of food, and put them into a horse drawn cart waiting outside the house. Mother told the owner to inform Benigna who was staying further down the road. The house we were then staying at was Boguslawskiego 19 in Przemysl. The official and the four soldiers came with us to make sure we got to the railway station where we could see empty cattle trucks were waiting.

It really was an incredible sight that met us. Hundreds of Polish families were arriving from all over Przemysl. Some had already arrived well before us. Others were coming in from all sides, each guarded by Russian soldiers, some in carts, some on lorries. There was panic. People were shouting, some were crying, little children not knowing what was happening. Mind you, their parents didn't know either. Fear spread like wild fire.

Soon we saw others that we had met before. There was our aunt Krzysia with her mother and son Ryszard who had just arrived; at least we would be together.

The soldiers put our belongings into one of the trucks. We were all told to get in. So this was going to be our 'first class compartment, Russian style'. Each cattle truck had wooden horizontal slats on both sides. Forty people were squashed into each truck. They put an old fashioned iron heater in the middle which had a chimney pipe going up to the top of the truck. That was the total furnishing of our 'cell', for that's what it was.

The official said with a sneering smile, *"Make yourselves at home, enjoy the journey!"* That farewell message told us to expect a long journey. No-one said where we were going. I don't expect the NKVD official knew either. The orders were simply to get all these people from their houses to the railway station and into the trucks.

All of a sudden we saw Benigna, rushing round the cattle trucks trying to find us; she was crying and wanted to come with us. She was obviously not on the list for deportation. Dear Benigna, my nanny, so wanted to stay with us that she begged the NKVD official and as a 'sweetener' gave him a beautiful watch. He quickly pocketed the watch and told her she could accompany us but she would have to hurry and collect her belongings from where she was living. Unfortunately, we never saw Benigna again, in fact I cannot even remember what she looked like – I was still only five years old at that time. Soon after she left, the cattle trucks were closed and bolted on the outside. Just after midday the train moved out of the station to start its journey, God only knew where and how long the journey would take. All we knew was that we were prisoners cooped up like cattle and obviously going East. East meant Siberia, East meant leaving Poland, East meant extremes of cold, pain, uncertainty, foreign lands and foreign people. We would be away from Poland, family and friends, its language, away from its very soul.

So the seven of us, that is we four and Aunt Krzysia's three, found ourselves places on the wooden slats. We quickly found some warm clothing to sit on and act as mattresses. We were not prepared with any other luxuries such as blankets or cushions. Each family had their corner and each jealously guarded their own space and, just like animals, there were arguments and quarrels if someone took a few more inches.

Our companions were a very mixed bunch of people. Some we knew, the majority we didn't know and didn't want to know. There were those that were selfish, others were self-important and self-opinionated, but there were also those of our countrymen who were selfless, generous and full of goodness.

Mother, in her account of this period, gave some examples of our companions on this journey. There was Mr and Mrs Z from Lwow in their 50s, he a businessman who had a chemists shop, stocky type with a small beard; she looked as if she liked her food – dumpy with a lot of makeup. She often took more food in a sneaky way. They had a daughter in her teens, a quiet girl who did not speak to anyone. Mrs Z was loquacious, liked to entertain others with her tales and show off her jewellery, while the daughter, Helena, was a violin player.

There was Mrs Cz from Krakow, aged about 60. She was a woman who wanted to be better off and tried very hard to please everybody. She wore rather colourful clothes, cheap but clean. Her husband was some kind of railway official.

There was also Mrs J. She and her 15 year old son Kaziu were from Warszawa. She was the wife of an army captain, who she believed was taken as a POW on the outskirts of Warszawa. She was a bit of a 'know-all' and used to tell everyone about their wonderful friends and the parties she attended. At other times she used to suddenly get very depressed, crying her eyes out. Her son was a nice looking boy of secondary school age. Maciej had some good chats with him.

Mrs K was about 35 and from Krakow. Her husband was a Major in a cavalry regiment. She hoped that he had either escaped to Romania or to Hungary. She was a generous and pleasant woman with whom Mother had long conversations. She had her mother with her who was in her late 50s. The mother was very religious and we saw her with her rosary most days.

The other man near us was Mr W. He was a little man in his late 60s with a bald head and shaky hands, very much working class. His wife, ten years younger with soiled clothes and slovenly. We all wondered why the Russians wanted to deport him until we found out later that he used to be an excellent chef in Poznan.

So there we were, forty 'oddballs' shut up in this cattle wagon prison. Everyone argued, everyone shouted a lot. At night there were people who prayed, others who cried and many who snored. Not a great time for sleeping.

We were given some water, barely enough for drinking, certainly not enough for washing; the smell of unwashed bodies was horrific.

The train went on and on. Soon we left the Polish countryside and were in the Ukraine. The train passed all towns and villages without stopping. A whole week went past before we were let out. We had been through Kiev and Kharkov and it was at Voronezh that they unbolted the doors. It was absolutely horrendous to be imprisoned in this way but nobody could do anything about it.

Once a day they gave us something to eat – one bucket of watery soup and usually 8-10 loaves of bread. That was supposed to feed 40 people. Everyone was hungry and thirsty most of the time. How did we manage? The children, myself included, got more than the adults. That's nature. There were some who grabbed at the bread and thereby left smaller portions to others. Like animals - the bigger you are, the quicker you are, the more you will grab – survival of the fittest. The two boys – Maciej and Ryszard – managed to get our quota sufficiently well. There were some that starved. Sometimes it looked like 'pigs at a trough' with everyone shouting, yelling, elbowing and pushing. Hunger makes people forget who they are. Society breaks down into inhumanity.

The train sometimes stopped near villages and people came out bringing milk, bread and sometimes even eggs. They were ordinary people, peasants, but good and generous. It amazed us; they knew we were Polish but they also knew that they and we were Slavs. There was one day when we stopped at a town station. Tota managed to get out and buy a map. We could now see that we were travelling further and further east. Soon we crossed the Volga river. How much further would the train go? Was our destination Siberia? There were many questions, but nobody to answer them. We felt wretched, desolate, crushed, in despair. It felt like the end of the world. But, as a child of five, well I probably thought it was an adventure, although the hunger made it an unpleasant adventure.

So what did these men and women do? They talked – could they have managed to avoid the situations in which they were in? The women gossiped, swapped stories, told of better times. They told each other where they came from. People played cards, patience, noughts and crosses, even chess. The men discussed politics and how the war was going. Some read books if they had them. The children made friends, looked out of the window or just looked bored. One of the men played on his mouth-organ. People joined in singing Polish songs. Another recited 'Pan Tadeusz'. One woman knew Russian and started a class. There was another woman who could draw quite well – she even did portraits. We all tried to forget our present circumstances. The nights were the worst - you miss your bed; the wooden racks were hard to lie on, the nights were cold and the noises around you did not exactly aid sleep. In fact nobody slept much. Did they dream? Yes, but not in their sleep.

Apart from the lack of food and the sleeping quarters, there was, let's call it, the comfort station which was actually just a bucket. A sort of screen was put around, made from someone's sheets. I am guessing there must have been a routine of 'use it, empty it' – out of the windows, how else?!

Poles by nature are a very clean people. Visit any Polish towns and you will never see any litter anywhere on the streets. So, although I do not remember, or take notice of these facts at my tender age, there must have been a general tidying and sweeping routine amongst the women.

As this was the latter part of April, the outside and therefore inside was relatively warm during the day. One night everyone woke up with a start when the old chimney from the stove came crashing down. Smoke billowed everywhere and the fire had to be put out.

Travelling through the flat countryside, occasionally the train stopped at a small station to take on water and coal. We were then allowed out to stretch our legs. Lying on the bare slatted boards like sardines, so close to each other that you could not even turn over, was unbearable so this was a great relief, albeit temporary.

Looking out of the windows, the landscape was mostly flat and featureless. There was the odd farm with a cow, pigs, chickens and sometimes a horse or two, the peasants trying to scratch a living from this dry land. In some areas there were large wheat or other grain fields, obviously managed by farm co-operatives.

It was shortly before our journey ended that the train went past the Ural Mountains which reach to a height of over 6,000 feet. It was then that our spirits really deflated; this was the end of the world. We realised we had reached Siberia.

So it was that after two weeks and thousands of miles, the train finally stopped. We had arrived at Kustanoi, a large station in Kazakhstan. This province, in the middle of Russia is part of Asia. It is sparsely populated and in 1940 had a population of 34 million in the provinces of Kazakhstan, Uzbekistan, Turkmenistan, Tadjikistan and Kirghizia. All of these provinces totalled 78 per cent of the whole of USSR. By 1937 USSR had become the world's foremost producer of agricultural machines, including tractors and combine harvesters. Tractors were making large scale agriculture possible; 'idle and virgin lands' were cultivated. Irrigation of arid land regions contributed immensely to the increase in production. Kazakhstan was beginning to be mined extensively. There were large deposits of copper, lead, zinc, tin, silver and gold. The mining we never saw; the enormous fields stretching to the horizon we did see - we were in the middle of them.

The date was 26th April 1940. After two weeks it did not seem to matter anymore where we finally arrived. We only wanted to get out of this prison. The continuous sitting or lying on the hard planks was not only uncomfortable but our bodies were full of sores and aches. When the soldiers finally opened the doors, everyone jumped down from the cattle trucks to straighten their legs and backs. We had been travelling for so long, we were now beyond caring what could happen to us.

We were ordered to board the waiting lorries and in these we travelled for six hours to a large Kolkhoz, its village was called Suvaluvka. A Kolkhoz is a term used to denote a number of farms run on a collective basis.

That night all the Poles from the train slept in the school house. The next day an official of some kind just said: *"Find your own place to stay".* One must remember that hardly any of us spoke Russian, apart from a few words. No-one helped. Everyone rushed around the village, asking the locals for any kind of accommodation. The locals were not at all willing to take in these foreigners who were unwashed, dirty and could not speak their language.

In fact the village was so full that the officials decided on the next day that we were to be transported to the neighbouring Kolkhoz called Dobrynovka. It was definitely smaller and poorer but the Russians were quite friendly towards us. We stayed in Dobrynovka for a month, sharing a home with another Polish family; a mother and her three children. Remember Aunt Krzysia, her mother and son were still with us. After a while we even thought of buying the house which cost 300 roubles. As an example a 'pud' (16 lbs) of flour cost 3 roubles and selling a gold watch could produce 450 roubles.

The living conditions were very primitive. The house possessed one room and a kitchen. The only furniture in the one room consisted of one bed and a bench. We laid out a thick rug on the floor for sleeping. Old Mrs Sliwinska, my Aunt's mother, was given the bed and the other six of us slept on the floor. The neighbours were friendly and nice people. Sign language was used in most cases. During the first fortnight they brought us lots of food, especially on one particular feast day celebrated by all the Russians. We were able to buy eggs, bacon, butter and fresh vegetables without too much trouble. I remember these days as of 'milk and honey' when compared with the amount of food we had later on.

Here we still had most of our possessions that we had brought with us from Przemysl. As we could not earn money by working, we had to barter with the Russians. As an example we bartered one of our shirts to earn ourselves 50 litres of milk.

It surprised us that there was not even a chapel in Dobrynovka. At one time there had been a chapel but it had been turned into a storehouse. The Russian people, especially the older ones, were very religious. In their huts they had many pictures of saints and icons which must have come from the church originally. There were no orthodox priests to be seen anywhere.

As we were the only Poles in Dobrynovka and longed to be amongst our own countrymen, Mother asked the NKVD official many times for permission to return to Suvaluvka. Finally he gave in and around

25th May we moved back there. Some friends of ours let us have a very nice hut for a rent of 50 roubles per month. Who the friend was and how he was the owner of this hut, I have no idea. Unfortunately, going through my Mother's story, there are lots of questions that I wish I could have asked but never did.

This little 'house' with two rooms and an adjacent kitchen, stood in the middle of the village, in the shade of a few tall trees. The heat in June and July was extreme, mostly 25-35°C. It was a dry heat with hardly ever any rain. We also had a fine garden and it quickly became a common meeting place for all the Polish families.

The next two and a half months were spent very happily for all seven of us. It was a palace in comparison to where we were to end up. We were amongst our own people, the people who came with us on the train. Even the Russians who lived in the village were now friendly towards us and no-one was forced to work. Tota and Maciej got very bored as, apart from borrowing books and learning Russian from the locals, there was not much to do.

There was a Polish woman who used to be a school teacher at one time. She was persuaded to start a class for the young people. It was not very successful as there were of course no books to use and also a lack of writing paper. She tried to teach Polish history, geography and literature but without any form of reference books; she had to give up after a month or so.

The summer months passed as we talked and reminisced about Poland, our houses, towns and villages. The Russian officials made various statements at odd times. They promised that we would eventually return to Poland. As we knew from experience, these officials were born liars so no-one actually believed them. However, as usual, people believed in dreams because it was natural and better to believe rather than not to believe.

There was always great excitement and rejoicing on the odd occasions when letters came from Poland. Once or twice a parcel even found its way to us. There is an interesting postcard written on 20th April 1940, so seven days after our deportation from Przemysl. It is written by Jozefa Plewkiewicz(grandmother) from our house in Warszawa (with two 5 pfennig Hindenburg German stamps and also two Polish stamps overprinted with General Gouvernement Swastikas on both with the German currencies of 6 and 12 pf. It is addressed to Stefan Dembinski, Tukor ucca 2, Budapest. She says,

"I sit in the kitchen in the mornings cooking a very small lunch such as a vegetable broth. A friend has brought me twelve packets of biscuits so it is very useful for someone that is ill. In the afternoon I work in the garden – for the last three days it has been lovely and warm. It is awful to think of the very hard and freezing weather we had last winter. A new currency came into being. All the old money has been taken away as it is worthless. Black marketeers buy dollars at 120 zloty to the dollar. Some people are starving while others have plenty – even too much. Yesterday Michal (Father's valet) *went to buy potatoes at 80 zloty a bag. These are scarce at this time. Much of the potato crop was frozen in the clamps outside. We are waiting for your wife's return. If only God would help them to return."*

On 16th July Maciej wrote a postcard from Kustanaiska Oblasc, Kurasuski Rejon, Suvaluvka Selsoviet, Pasiolek, USSR to Stanislaw Dembinski (our uncle) c/o Mr Hope Johnstone, Peking, China. The message has already been given previously. A similar card was written by our Mother to Stanislaw on 29th July 1940. Both cards would not have been received by our uncle as he died in Peking on 1st August.

During all this time in Suvaluvka we did not get news of what was happening in the rest of the world and in particular how the war was going. We had no idea when Hitler invaded Belgium and Holland (10th May) or Denmark and Norway (9th April). Neither did we know about the disaster of the British troops and their evacuation from Dunkirk (1st June), that Italy declared war on Britain (11th June) or that France capitulated on 22nd June.

We knew nothing of the Polish Government in Exile having to leave Paris for London. The new Polish President, Wladyslaw Raczkiewicz, General Sikorski, the Prime Minister and Commander -in-Chief, all arrived in London on 21st June 1941, one day before France fell.

The only news around Suvaluvka was the kind that said: "Did you hear that the Germans have been defeated?" or "that Britain has given up". It was gossip, handed from one to another. Often it was so incredible that nobody believed it. From time to time a Russian newspaper arrived, printed locally in a neighbouring town. The Russians seemed to live life from one day to the next and did not appear to be interested in anything that happened outside that little village.

In our garden we grew vegetables and spent the time weeding and generally finding something to do to occupy our lives. Never having been a gardener, Mother acquired knowledge, especially from the house owner's mother-in-law, who became a good friend. It is obvious to me now that Mother was able to converse quite well in Russian, as she and the old Babushka, who was old enough to remember the Tsarist times, would chat sitting in our garden. She helped us many times, often bringing little presents of food secretly tucked into her apron so that her daughter-in-law would not see it. She would often sit down and listen to our tales from Poland and then reminisce about the pre-1917 times. She was so attached to Mother that she made her promise to write to her when we returned to Poland.

Sundays here were like Sundays everywhere at that time. Everyone put on their best clothes; the girls put on their finest and very colourful dresses and then strolled around the village showing off to the young men. Both Maciej and Ryszard were looked out for and when they were seen, the Russian girls put on their most engaging smiles. It reminded us to some extent of our Polish villages on similar Sunday afternoons.

In early August the resident NKVD official often came to tell us that we would soon be moved to another place. He promised that it would be a better village where everyone would be given their own house and where each Polish member could make a good living out of the work given to him. As usual everyone believed in good faith. What an unpleasant surprise we were soon to have.

So here we were - reasonably happy, healthy and with enough to eat. The summer was hot still. Most of the Russians in the village were now friendly towards us. Could this 'promised land' that the NKVD official was talking about be better than this? We did of course have periods of depression, mainly because we were homesick for the luxuries which we were used to in Warszawa. After all, living thousands of miles away in the centre of Asia amongst foreign Slavs was very different from the life we were accustomed to. Having time on our hands, we planned and dreamed like people do everywhere. Being naïve, we dreamed and longed to get out of this village and have our own little house in paradise.

Reference at this stage should be made to Wlodzimierz Dembinski. He was Father's younger brother, born at Nowe Sioto in the Galicia region of Poland on 20th February 1889, so two years younger than Father. His sister was Mucha or Maria Jakubowska and she was six years younger than Wlodzimierz. He was a Colonel in the Polish Army, as well as being a Doctor at Law. He married Krystyna (Krzysia) Sliwinska. They had one son, Ryszard (Rys) and of course it was Aunt Krzysia and cousin Rys who travelled with us across Poland to Przemysl and were exiled with us in Asia. On being de-mobbed in 1947 in England, Wlodziu (diminutive) lived with his wife in Balham, South London at 43 Carmenia Road. At the age of 19 their son, Ryszard, joined the Armoured Cavalry Regiment in the Middle East, fighting in Italy and later in Belgium in 1944-45.

Our uncle Wlodzimierz, as already mentioned, met Father while he was on his way from Hungary to France. Unfortunately there are no letters from him but there are two envelopes from 10, Rue de Baudin in Parthenay-Deux-Sevre in France. The first is addressed to Father in Budapest, date of postage 1 May 1940. It is stamped 'ouvert par l'autorite militaire' (opened by the military authority) at Niort on 5th May 1940. The date mark shows it was received in Budapest on 10th May 1940.

The second envelope, also from the same address in France written by Wlodzimierz, has date of postage 13th May 1940 with 'Censure Militaire', no French stamps – marked F.M. (franc Militaire). This time it is sent to Father (who by then had escaped from internment in Hungary) at Hotel de Danube, 58 Rue Jacob, Paris. It has a stamped slogan – 'Touristes-Visitez Parthenay et la Batine'.

I would imagine that Wlodzimierz left France for Switzerland, a neutral country, before France surrendered to the Nazis on 22nd June. Two thousand soldiers of the Polish Rifle Division crossed over to Switzerland, together with 15,000 French soldiers. All were interned and placed into camps where they spent the rest of the war.

There are two envelopes from him from Elgg, Winterthur, Switzerland. One date-stamped 23rd January 1943 and the other 8th May 1943. Both were opened by Examiner and Commande der Wehrsmacht. Both have a smeared chemical test for secret writing diagonally across the envelopes. One was written to Father at 91 Eton Hall, London NW3, the other to Mother at the same address.

CHAPTER 5

TO HELL AND BACK - TOCHKA ET ALIA

14TH AUGUST 1940 – 10TH SEPTEMBER 1941

I now return to Mother's account of our darkest year in our deportation into Asiatic Russia.

On the 14th August 1940 we were finally ordered to assemble with all our belongings. On the following day we said our farewells to everyone we had got to know. With our hopes high, we were loaded onto lorries and off we went on this journey; some went one way, others another way. Our lorry continued monotonously hour after hour. We travelled through an empty, wild and more savage steppe. The steppe was extremely flat and very arid at this hot time of the year. Nothing was cultivated, there were no trees, just tall dry grasses.

We came across less and less villages. Sometimes, at the sound of the lorry's horn, peculiar and half savage people appeared. These were the Kozaks of the Asian steppes. They stared at us in a wild way. They originated from Mongolia and were traditionally nomadic tribes. Their language was unfamiliar and very strange to the European or Slav ear. We looked at them in fear and horror. The difference between what we left behind in Suvaluvka was as chalk from cheese.

The NKVD official who was escorting us told us: *"They are your friends now. They are also your masters. Do as they tell you."* We now realised that the stories they kept telling us about the Utopia we would go to were a pack of lies. A sudden fear gripped us and that fear filled us with dread of what lay ahead of us. We could not be further from civilisation. We were stepping over into the unknown abyss. Was it this hell that was to be our new abode? The further we travelled, hour upon hour, the grimmer it looked and the more depressed we became.

After eight hours' travelling through the endless steppe with hardly any habitation now, the lorries finally came to a halt in the so-called 'Central'. This was a kind of headquarters from which this part of the steppe was managed. We were directed to wait in the local school and here we stayed for several days before they decided where to send us.

So, by about the 19th August, we got into the lorries once again and were transported to the 'Firm', a lower degree of the agricultural system in Kazakhstan. The next day a young Polish boy arrived with a wooden cart harnessed with oxen. His description of our final destination was horrific. He just said: 'It could not be worse'.

The seven of us - Mother with us three children, Aunt Krzysia with her mother and Ryszard, climbed onto the wagon. After about twenty kilometres trundling along in the cart across the steppe, we finally arrived at our destination. This was Tochka, the lowest rung of the human ladder, a Sovkhoz or state farm in the middle of the so-called 'virgin lands' which had only recently been ploughed/cultivated.

Tochka consisted of two larger huts occupied by Kozaks, two long cow sheds and one row of five huts all joined together. What a sight to behold! The young lad told us that we could use two of these huts. We looked at them with horror; one had a completely ruined roof – if you could call it a roof! The other was in an even worse condition with hardly a wall standing. To a Kozak, a hut should have only four basic fundamentals: 4 walls, one roof, one door and one window. Well the first one had the walls but none of the other basics. We decided that all seven of us would have to use the one hut. That was an easy decision but the next problem was that it needed repairing then and there before we could use it.

So the first day was taken up repairing our humble dwelling, or what there was of it. Everyone went out onto the steppe near the river to cut down reeds. The horizontal lengths of wood were still remaining on the roof so all we had to do was to interlace them with the reeds. We hoped that we would not get any wind, otherwise the reeds would disappear off the roof. Later we would find a way of ensuring the reeds were secure.

Thank goodness it was summer and warm. Having made ourselves a makeshift roof over our heads, it was then time to reconnoitre the other empty ruined huts and cowsheds. We managed to find an old door and old windows in one of the cowsheds and also old wooden boards which we could use for sleeping. The floor of the huts was just beaten earth, covered with dirt of all shades and colours and mainly of the brown dung variety.

The local Kozaks then woke up to the fact that we were stealing all these articles from their sheds. A great fight took place, with Maciej and Ryszard giving them much Polish curses and damnations. The Kozaks were doing the same in their own language. Neither one nor the other understood a word of what was being said, however the boys somehow managed to win this battle as all the bits and pieces got dragged to our hut. They were much more precious to us and I believe the Kozaks understood this in the end and gave in. So now we had a roof, a door and a window. These were the fundamentals. The only furniture we possessed was an old iron bed which Mother managed to buy in Suvaluvka and it somehow managed to arrive with us on the cart. There was no way of making any furniture as there were no trees on the steppe so therefore no wood. Even if we had managed to obtain wood, we had no saw, hammer or nails.

The first day over, we had to somehow find a way of eating something and secondly find something to lie on for sleeping. Who decided where and on what we slept, I do not know. Sixty five years later, Maciej drew me a plan of how everyone was 'accommodated'. Remember that there were seven of us. There was an old cooking range, rusty and dirty, on which Auntie Krzysia and Ryszard slept,

Babcia Sliwinska on one wooden board, Tota on another wooden board, Maciej on a suitcase and finally Mother and I on the iron bed. And this was how we existed for a year. Thinking about it in later years – how did we survive this 'Hell hole'?

On the second day and into the autumn we got to know the system of building these huts. It was very simple and primitive; clay was collected from the steppe, then mixed with ox dung and moulded by hand into bricks. These were then left in the hot sun to bake dry. The bricks were then used to build the walls. The construction of the roof consisted of positioning two wooden props and one parallel beam on top. Reeds were then thatched across the beam. Finally soil was put on as a covering which then baked solid in the summer sun. Having built the walls with baked bricks, they were then hand-plastered with a mix of clay and dung. The final refinement was to use clay by itself to give the outside of the walls a smooth appearance. All this was done by hands, which got very sore.

The floor was beaten down so that the clay became hard and flat. The windows may have had glass in them but certainly in the winter would normally have been closed with some kind of shutters. In the hot summers, it was always dusty and difficult to keep clean, while in the harsh winter it was freezing cold and wet. The thatched roof never kept out the rain and snow. The roof could easily collapse under the weight of snow.

Kazakhstan was enormous, being 1,560,000 sq kms, approximately 12% of the whole of USSR and roughly one third as large as the USA. It had a population then of 3.5 million – amazingly small for its size. Not surprisingly 60% of it was steppe pasture land growing cereals, sunflower and tobacco. It stretched from the Caspian Sea in the south to the Altai Mountains in the north and it bordered the Sinkiard province of China.

Tochka was in Eastern Kazakhstan, right in the middle of this huge steppe. The steppe stretched flat to the horizon. In the summer the sun burned the steppe so that it looked grey, lifeless and pitiful to behold. When lightning struck, the tinder grass caught fire. Even now I remember seeing these fires, which stretched right across the horizon; very frightening. The only way the fires were extinguished was with thunder storms bringing rain. Thank God the wild fire never got close to us.

When we arrived in Tochka it was still mid-Summer. Apart from the few Kozaks, the place was dead. No animal moved, no birds sang, there were no flowers, bushes or trees. The colour was ashen, grey, brown. Not a green shoot or leaf anywhere. Even the flies were in short supply. All was desolation. We were intimidated and frightened. Was this what the surface of the moon looked like? Even the moon has some hills on it. It was a blessing that all seven of us were still together, otherwise there was no communication with the outside world as we did not have a radio. There was certainly no communication with any of the Kozak people – at the beginning anyhow – due mainly to their strange language which was presumably some kind of a mixture of Chinese and Russian.

Although I have just described the steppe as dead, this was during the day. It was during the night that it came to life. The wolves howled – a piercing, chilling sound which shattered the silence of the night. In the first few nights we could not get to sleep; the howling sounded so malevolent and savage.

Tochka was the smallest of any sovkhoz, which in Soviet terminology means a state farm. Near this 'village' of seven huts and two cowsheds was a very deep gorge, at the bottom of which was a very small salty river. When we arrived, the river was nearly dried up and looked more like a stream. In some summers apparently it dried up completely so that one could walk across it. The water stank horribly but this water was the only source for us. It was this salty, filthy water that we had to use for drinking, cooking and washing. The only way to get this water was to climb down into the ravine and then carefully bring it up again without spilling too much on the rough hillside. Once brought up, it had to be skimmed of its filth, then boiled and finally cooled for washing ourselves and our clothes. We dreamed of water that came out of taps – turn the tap and out it comes, pure and delicious! A bath full of it, a shower with water streaming down……….but these were only mirages. We had to adapt to the environment in which we found ourselves, what else could we do? We had to keep clean, to drink and to cook with it. The Kozaks got their water supply from a neighbouring village. Occasionally they gave us some and it was like drinking the best champagne.

There were four Kozak families living in Tochka in their two long huts. Being Islamic, the older generation kept strictly to their religious rites but, as so often happens, the young were normally not at all religious. The women usually wore the traditional dress, which consisted of long colourful trousers tucked into high boots. The sleeves of their dresses were very wide. A long jacket to the knees and, for the older women, a wide stiff scarf as headgear completed their costume. The dresses were sometimes very rich in colour and very beautiful. The men on the other hand, dressed very shabbily. They also wore their trousers tucked into high leather boots, a shirt hanging some way to their knees and a leather jerkin. They always wore high fur hats, both in the extreme cold of winter and the heat of summer.

We became very conscious of the Kozak's family life. Both the women and the men cared much about their children. Both spent time playing with them and never left them alone. Very early on the tiny tots walked with them, imitating their father and mother. We saw them in the cowsheds helping with the milking, clearing out the dung. In the house they were always with their mother cooking the meals.

The children's birthdays were always celebrated in great style. Food was plentiful and all the neighbours were invited and made very welcome. The children were given money as presents. Everyone sang to please the mother who, fearing being bewitched, hid the birthday child jealously from everyone. The Kozaks had many customs and traditions. Mostly they seemed strange and weird to us but of course we came from another planet a thousand miles away. Language was a big barrier so bartering for food was often impossible apart from using sign language. They often tried to swindle us during these exchanges of our belongings, mostly clothes, and their food.

In their own group they were very honest and the not-so-poor gave and helped the very poor whenever they could. So, although they appeared to us a wild tribe, in a lot of ways they were civilised with their own style and manners. They should not have been blamed for thinking that we had little culture. Their judgement was formed on the basis of the possessions people had. We had nothing. They were also convinced that we had been deported for some unknown crime that we had committed. I wonder what they thought we had been accused of. Most probably they imagined that we all stole a cow, perhaps a horse or a pig. I cannot believe that they thought one of us might have committed murder.

The old people were usually illiterate. The young went to school. Where was this school? I have no idea how far the nearest village was from Tochka. We were not allowed to go there but it must have been within horse and cart travelling distance, perhaps 10-12 miles. Those children had school books but no-one had any books which they could read for pleasure – that went for the older generation as well. By law they had to send the children to school, but for many reasons, much of the time they stayed by their parents' side. There were myriad excuses: too far to take them there and back, the weather was too cold/too hot, they had to help on the farm, the parents could not afford to pay for their education.

The living conditions of the Kozaks were primitive to say the least. They had few machines and even fewer tools. They sat on wooden boards which acted well enough as their beds. They ate out of a common bowl using either a common spoon or often using their hands.

The day's work started at sunrise for them. No breakfast was eaten, just tea in bowls to warm them up. The first meal of the day was consumed around midday. The usual meal was 'lepioshka', a kind of bread pancake similar to an Indian chapatti. Much tea was drunk from the samovar. Sugar was a luxury so it was only used on special occasions as a treat, such as birthdays or festive days. If there was a shortage of tea, hot water with milk was the substitute. Supper was at about 5pm and consisted of 'lapsho' – a type of lasagne boiled in milk with a sprinkling of lumps of mutton, or on special occasions, horse meat.

In the summer's heat, the meat – beef, mutton, horse or pork – was dried outside. Before it dried it became rotten with flies settling on it and so the maggots got there first. The Kozaks' favourite dish was wheatcorn shallow fried in suet. We prepared and ate this delicacy ourselves and personally I remember enjoying it. At least it filled our stomachs. A great delicacy for the Kozaks was sheep's milk put into bowls to make it sour. We also found it very delicious and nourishing – when we could obtain it – we called it 'Champagne'. From the curd they made an excellent white cheese which was then dried as hard as Parmesan. They called it 'Kurt'. All our family loved it.

The cooking during the summer was done outside the house. The cooker was very basic and elementary. A hole was made in the hard ground, and stones placed into and above it. As there was no wood, the fuel used was 'Kiziak' (in our language 'cowpats'). For lighting the dried Kiziak, we used the very dry grass or weeds. This grass was called 'topka' and grew to a height of six feet on the steppe. It was really strong and was the thickness of a man's arm.

Both the grass/weeds and the cowpats were collected in late summer and autumn to dry out the moisture. Both were then put into stacks inside the hut for winter use. Once the winter came, the cooking had to be done inside the hut. The 'Kiziak' never really dried completely and soon became damp. It was therefore very difficult to light this 'fuel'. When it finally decided to light, with more and more 'topka' being applied, it produced the most obnoxious smell. It burnt the eyes and made all your clothes stink - imagine a bonfire inside the hut but not using wood, only dried manure. It should be remembered that there was no chimney in the huts. When the snows came, the windows were blocked by the drifts of snow which reached above the roof of the hut. The only exit was to build a tunnel in the snow and so reach fresh air and ventilation. I wonder how we managed not to choke to death on the smoke.

The agricultural year only began in the Spring. When the snows had melted, the soil took its time to dry out. The fields were ploughed shallowly, harrowed and then the sowing begun. In these conditions the fight against the weeds was almost impossible as both the corn and the weeds emerged together.

The agricultural machines were mostly new. By 1937 USSR became the world's foremost producer of these, including huge combine harvesters. By 1940 half a million tractors were making large scale agriculture possible. For example, from 1913 to 1941 agricultural production doubled; completely new areas were opened up in the Urals, Siberia and Kazakhstan. The irrigation of arid steppe land contributed immensely to the increase in production. The area of irrigated land almost doubled between 1913 and 1940. In the area that we were living, they had not yet heard about irrigation so the corn suffered.

To give these machines to the Kozaks was one thing, but to maintain them was another. Insufficient people were trained to mend them and generally look after them. In front of the smithy were numerous machines sitting idle or being stripped of useful parts to mend or service others. The colossal combine harvesters, cutting several metres wide, were very much more superior to the Polish ones.

The harvest of corn was unimaginable in quantity and quality in good seasons. The biggest problem during the harvest was lack of a workforce. A great deal of the grain was wasted because it could not be gathered in time. One could see fields of ripe corn being battered by strong winds and rain. You could not make comparisons with the hay harvest of the steppes. In the Spring, the steppe was green with new grass. I have never forgotten the kaleidoscope presented to the eye of wild tulips of every hue as far as one can see, and the fragrance was out of this world.

The tractors with their mowing machines behind cut down the hay in swathes. The scorching sun dried the hay instantly and it was gathered by other machines pulled by oxen. The hay was then piled into large and very high carts, again driven by oxen and then put into very large stacks. Everyone except me helped with gathering the hay harvest. Mother, Maciej, Ryszard and Tota would always remember the smell of the hay drying. Also they would remember even more how much sweat was lost working out there.

The oxen were tough and hard looking, two of them to a cart and one person to control them. An expert handler could make the oxen go in the right direction. They were made to work by constant shouting and use of a long whip of plaited leather called a 'Knut'. The boys got to be pretty good drivers of these 'beasts of burden'. It was a thirsty business both for the drivers and for the oxen, so water had to be provided but no-one was allowed more than a few minutes for breaks. The smell of the sweating beasts was a very strong odour.

There were times when, on account of the very hot summer, the steppe grass dried before it could be cut. Each sovkhoz had to fulfil the desired 'norm' or quota. If the amount of hay gathered was insufficient for winter feeding of the oxen and cattle, the animals died. In the harsh winter of 1940/41, when we were there, 75% of the cattle died of starvation. Although the Kozaks butchered the dead animals, there was not much meat on them; they looked like skeletons.

The problem of work in Russia was rather difficult for us deportees. It was compulsory for everyone over the age of 14 to work, so I was the only one who was excluded. Tota, Maciej and Ryszard worked very hard indeed. During the sowing in the spring of 1942 and later during the harvesting of hay and the crops, they worked for sixteen hours a day. Usually they went to work before dawn and returned back by moonlight. The pay depended on achieving the 'norm'. The norm was the amount of work expected to be completed in a day as directed by the agricultural officials. None of the workers was told what the norm was to be on any particular day. It varied from one day to another, so when the officials decided it was reached, the workers were allowed to go home. As the fields being harvested were often a long way off, our lot would be taken back to Tochka on a cart and oxen. In the summer months, work was organised in groups or 'brigades'. Often these brigades worked even further afield and too long to enable them to return to the sovkhoz at the end of the day. In this case the workers slept in the fields or in special wagons. The mosquitos had a feast, biting them terribly.

Food was given to them once a day but it was not a free handout; the workers had to pay for it by deduction from their monthly wages. The ration of a kilo of bread per day was very useful as it could be saved by Maciej, Ryszard and Tota to be brought back for the rest of the family.

The best paid workers were those who drove the tractors and combine harvesters. Women were the worst paid. Women, like Mother, who had children to look after, were given work near the sovkhoz. The workers were given special cards which allowed them to buy some products at official prices. Those who did not or could not work, like Babcia Sliwinska, had to pay the current market prices which were much higher. One person could buy eight kilos of flour for himself per month and also four kilos per child per month. This was of course the most important and staple food for baking and cooking.

There was still an awful lot of land not under the plough and completely wild. The soil was very rich, more like gold. Probably it was rich because it had not been cultivated for years or perhaps ever. The whole Stalin concept was to produce 'more' but because there were not enough workers, not enough machines – or if there were they stood idle getting rusty – the year's norm was never achieved. They were rusty because there were insufficient trained engineers to cope with the maintenance of them. The Kozaks were rather lazy and disliked any sort of work outside their family commitment. When they did have to work, they did not really care how well they performed the tasks. Mainly the fault, as in any society, was with the officials and administrators who were very hard on the workers. Instead of giving them some kind of 'carrot', they gave out punishments for every kind of small offence, even imprisoning them.

As mentioned previously, the 'Firm' was at the top end of the agricultural system. The 'Kolkhoz' was a term used for a collection of farms and basically was middle rung of the ladder, while the 'sovkhoz' was the lowest in the system, ie Tochka.

Each 'firm' was responsible for breeding either dairy or beef cattle. There were others who specialised in horses, sheep or pigs. Tochka being the lowest in rank by a long chalk, was sent all the cattle that contracted TB. Maciej was often given the job of looking after them. His main occupation was therefore as a cow-boy, but not as in America. In America they had horses to round up the cows. Maciej, being without a horse, soon learnt all the Kozak words needed to shout and scream at the cows.   A whip of plaited leather came in handy as well.

In Dobrynowka, the Kolkhoz we stayed in initially, they bred horses. There were about 200 mares with foals, as well as four stallions. They fed out on the steppe most of the year and were only rounded up at night to be put into stables.   The wonderful sight of the galloping horses returning for the night was not easy to forget. The earth shook every evening under their hooves and the air vibrated from the neighing of the stallions and foals.

The Autumn of 1940 approached rapidly at Tochka. The days became shorter and the evening darkness became terribly long. As we had no light inside the huts, there was nothing we could do. The harvest had been gathered so everyone was 'home'. We, the outcasts, were given the worst jobs. One of those was rubbing the clay on the walls of the cowsheds. Soon everyone's hands got very sore from the clay which had sharp stones in it.
During these evenings, the stove smoked terribly, making us cough and our eyes water continuously.   Even though it was cold outside,

we had to leave the door open while cooking. We were always short of 'kiziak'. Often we had to barter some of our possessions in order to have this priceless fuel to cook on and keep us from being frozen alive. Years later, this seems absurd, ridiculous! We were exchanging our prized possessions for dung!

By joining the co-operative, Mother could buy goods at government prices. Twice a month a large cart, looking like a gypsy caravan, used to arrive at Tochka. We could buy a rationed amount of flour and sugar. Of course, we were the last to be allowed to buy anything and inevitably the goods ran out before it came to our turn. Salt, the precious commodity, always ran out before we could buy it.

Due to the shortages of food, we all became ill with dysentery throughout that autumn and winter. There was no meat or fruit and seldom any vegetables. One cannot imagine the complications and privations of going 'to do one's business' outside; the 'privy' was not only outside but also without any walls or roof. You often squatted in temperatures of -40 °C and in the snow. You learnt that if you did not want frostbite, your squatting was done in record time. No toilet paper, no newspapers but plenty of snow.

Constant requests for us to be transferred to the 'Firm' were always refused. One day the manager of the 'centre' came to visit Tochka. Mother complained to him about the awful state of our hut. By now the roof was leaking constantly. He just lost his temper and started to shout: *"Don't think you will ever see your beloved Warszawa again. This is your Warszawa and here you will end your days".* You can imagine how we felt.

Our primitive neighbours used to annoy us with their curiosity and persistence in examining all our 'worldly' possessions; sometimes they would stay for hours in our hut so that we were forced to show them some object or other. If they fancied any particular thing, they would invent all kinds of ways to force us to sell it to them. The easiest way for them to do this was to refuse to sell us grain. Especially noted for this was one family renowned in the kolkhoz as the worst thieves. Mother could have chosen to live in a better hut with a Kozak family but it was definitely better to live in the worst hut than have the inquisitive half-savages share space with us.

We became overjoyed when we received a letter or two from Poland. We even got two parcels with some of our warm clothes. This was an outstanding feat considering how far we were, not only from a town but from civilisation itself. The post was amazingly efficient and nothing was ever stolen. Those two parcels lifted our spirits no end and somehow gave us some hope for the winter to come.

Unfortunately none of the letters or postcards arriving in Tochka were kept, nor for that matter letters/postcards written by Mother to relatives in Poland. It would have provided interesting reading. However, some correspondence between other members of the family during this period was kept.

There were one or two postcards written to Father from Poland. He was then stationed in Scotland. The first postcard written in the Autumn of 1940 was from Wanda Grocholska, residing at Batorego 22/4, Krakow. This lady was the sister of Krystyna Dembinska and had connections with Zozia (Zonka) Dembinska from Jaslo, which is not far from Krakow. It is addressed to East 67 Street, Room 305, New York 151 but Father was never in New York. Both this card and the other three described later were addressed to Father in a neutral country. The USA did not declare war on Germany until the Japanese attack at Pearl Harbour in Hawaii on 7th December 1941.

This latter postcard was written on 5th November 1940, (the postcard was Polish but the Germans overprinted it 'Post-Karte') and had a printed Polish stamp which was then overprinted with German currency and a horrible eagle and swastika obliterate the stamp. There are also three General Gouvernement stamps cancelled Krakow 4. It was sent Airmail and by registered post. To begin with it went to Uber Bahupostamt, Frankfurt/Main, which I would conclude would be the chief post office in Germany dealing with mail originating from conquered countries and written to a neutral country. There are receiving postmarks of New York Y Division (Registration) dated 17 December. It is addressed to Father as Mister Stefan Dembinski. The person receiving the postcard in Room 304 presumably knew both the identity and the address to which it should be sent on (Scotland). I must wonder when it would have finally reached him.

This card from Wanda Grocholska is interesting to read:

"*Dear Stefan, Zonka(Zosia) sent your address to Antoni* (which I presume is the husband of Marina Sliwinska – see Marina's letter to come). *We are taking the opportunity to let you know that Mother* (Mrs Sliwinska) *as well as Marysia* (our Mother), *Krzysia and all the children are still in Asia. They are healthy, they lack shoes and warm clothes. They write less often and there are less chances of sending them money. They work hard and it is easy to understand that their living standards are awful. From their postcards, one can deduce that they are horribly afraid of the coming winter and they are losing all hope of ever getting back home. As you are in New York, we are sending their address to you. You must get them out from there by bringing them to you through the services of the Red Cross. Anyway you have to help them in any way you can. There is nothing new with us. We are well, as is your mother* (Michalina) *and sister* (Zofia) . *We are terribly depressed about the loss of our nearest and dearest.*"

The address in Asia was then given:
"*Kustanajskaja Oblasc, Kurasuski Rejon, Kuszmirinskij Sowhoz, Farma No 4*
Janka and Ewa are also in Asia (some kind of cousins if I remember correctly). *We don't have their address. Perhaps something can be done for them.*"

On 11th November 1940 a similar postcard was sent to Father, this time from Marina Sliwinska (sister of Krystyna Dembinska) who is also a resident of Krakow at Bandurski Str 34. An interesting fact here – Maria Jakubowska or Mucha wrote from this address on 26th January 1946. As she died in Krakow in 1966, I wonder whether she came to live here. Before arriving in New York, this postcard has a received postmark of San Juan PR dated 29 November 1940. Does PR represent Puerto Rico? If so, this is off the direct route. Perhaps the plane temporarily stopped there for some reason. The receiving postmarks are of New York on 2 December 1940 and on the back another of New York on 12 January 1940. Possibly they had difficulty in tracing the recipient, ie Stefan Dembinski. The message on this card is very similar to the first, saying that they received our address in Asia from Father's Mother (Michalina Dembinska).

These two letters to Father, who was in Scotland, contained vital information regarding our whereabouts in Asia. I have an actual letter written by Father on 16th December 1940 from Edinburgh to a colleague of his, saying that he is very lonely and hopes that the weather would be reasonable so that he could walk on the local hills on his own. He says *'In this way I can exert myself and thereby be able to find some sleep at night.'* So for the past eight months he had not known what had happened to us after being deported from Przemysl on 13th April.

There are a couple of postcards from Michalina Dembinska to her son (Father) sent from Jaslo in November 1940. The first one is sent to New York, as above with similar Wehrmacht censor marks.

The postcard's message is:

"My dearest Stefan, It made me very happy to receive news from you and your whereabouts, that you are in good hands and we don't need to worry about you. God have mercy on us and He looks after all of us, so I don't worry. Don't you worry about the children and their mother. Have faith. We all pray here and I am sure they will all return home well and happy. Everything is alright with us. Zosia and I have courage. Marysia's address was sent to me by Antoni Sliwinski so I am writing to them at once."

The other postcard from Jaslo is written by Michalina Dembinska to Mrs Macmillan c/o M Biskupcki at another neutral country – Portugal. It is addressed to Rue Amoreivas 163, Lisbon. It thanks her for the parcels which took some time to arrive, however they were received in a fine condition. It asks the whereabouts of Mr Maciejewicz, which could have been a pseudonym for Father. The card has the usual 'Obercommando der Wehrmacht' control mark. It also has a couple of receiving postmarks of Lisbon dated 29 January 1940. It was obviously redirected to Father. The address in Lisbon could have been a Polish embassy or consulate.

* * * *

I now return to Mother's memories of the autumn of 1940 and the winter of 1940/41......

In November the snows started. Our little hut was no protection against the Siberian winter. Soon the drifting snow, carried by the vicious blizzard called a 'buran' covered the hut completely. The snow was about 8-12 ft deep. In order to get out of the hut, we had to tunnel our way from the door to the top of the snowdrift. Because the gradient had to be slight, the length of the tunnel was about 30ft. It was easy to get out the first day when the snow was still soft, but it froze during the night, making it very slippery. The upward slope was about a 20 degree angle, so it was devilishly difficult and dangerous climbing to the top and even worse when going back down. The method of digging yourself out was somewhat similar to that used in the tunnels dug by POWs in WW2 when escaping from Prisoner of War Camps. The biggest problem was getting rid of the snow. The only way was to pack the extra snow to the sides of the tunnel. Unfortunately this meant the walls when frozen turned to walls of ice. Soon the tunnel surface was also a solid smooth ice.

Most of the time it was pitch dark in the hut, both during the day and night. We were living exactly like moles. We allowed ourselves some light once a day when the meagre food was being prepared. The light came from a wick stuck in a bottle filled with oil. Sometimes we tried to dig the snow down to the windows but most of the time it was a futile exercise as the drifting snow soon covered up the holes. Anyhow the outside was just as bad. Freezing, with the temperature averaging -30°C and the sky was nearly black during the day. We wished we were bears who could go to sleep in the burrow and sleep through the cold winter.

To illustrate what a 'buran' was like, I give here Mother's description:

"The boys, Maciej and Ryszard went out one day before dawn to work in the cowsheds. These were about 200 yards from our hut. The snow swirled with the force of the wind, whipping it up into their faces. After a short time they could not see more than a few feet in front of them. They became completely disorientated. All of a sudden they fell into the deepest snow and could not get out. The more they struggled, the deeper they fell through the new snow. After a couple of hours they lost all hope of getting out or being found alive. The temperature was its usual -40°C. The 'buran' kept on endlessly with more and more snow falling. Little by little their strength sapped away. It was useless shouting for help. Nobody would have heard within a few feet anyway. They began to pray. At last they saw a light; a Kozak had come on his way to the cowshed carrying an oil lantern. They shouted at the top of their voices. Fortunately the man heard them and helped them out of the deep drift. They could hardly put one foot in front of the other as they were literally frozen, very nearly to death."

The only water was obtained from melting the snow. This luxury was only used for cooking purposes. Washing was quite impossible in these freezing conditions. Soap was another luxury used only on special occasions. Lice and fleas were rife; we could have been living in the Stone Age.

Our food now only consisted of flour. Mother scrupulously counted out four cupful's for each day. Remember this was for the seven of us. From this ration, a hot soup was made as well as a kind of bread pancake, both cooked on cinders. This was our 'daily bread', our only nourishment.

We still had a few possessions with which to barter. In this way we managed to get some grain from the Kozaks. At first it was wheat and, when that ran out, it was only barley. To give an example of the barter exchange, I will include here Mother's own words:

"A silver fox fur or a gold bracelet rated in exchange a bucketful of grain. The grain had to be ground in hand mills which were also hired at a price from the local Kozak. From experience we knew that if we wanted to grind a handful of grain, we had to turn the two stones sixteen times. The handmills were so primitive that we had to sit on the ground to operate them." After 70 odd years I personally still remember them!

We all became very thin and looked greyish-yellow. I suffered the worst, having now very little warm clothing and due to the lack of any nutritious food such as vegetables and fruit, I suffered with sores which were full of pus – a form of avitaminosa. We had hardly any medicine by now. The only way to keep it at bay was by washing with hot water and soap. Prayer was the other alternative. I suppose living in a refrigerator helped because somehow or other the sores healed.

Mother asked me a few days before Christmas what I wanted most as a present; my answer was: *'Perhaps I could have a piece of bread?'* Not a toy, not an orange, not a sweet, simply a piece of bread – and that was something that Mother could not find for me. But Christmas was some way off yet.

Maciej and Ryszard worked in the cowsheds all that bitter winter. The Kozak girls milked the cows and, although it was forbidden, they sometimes gave them a jug of milk to take home. The milk was of course not treated. After 5 months of working amongst these filthy animals and in stinking clothes, which could not be washed in these freezing temperatures, Maciej got terrible chilblains on his hands and feet. They gave him so much suffering that he had to lie in bed for weeks. Mother did not have any bandages for the sores that opened up, or if she had she would not have been able to wash them anyway as we had a constant lack of water, soap or disinfectant.

When falling ill in these conditions, it was very difficult to get back to health. There were no medicines, not even basic ones. The alternatives were three-fold; you had to be strong in mind and body, secondly you had to trust to luck, finally you prayed to God.

Religion did play a part. Being strong Roman Catholics, we had faith in our God and the Madonna of Czestochowa, or as she is known in the wider world, 'The Black Madonna'. Sometimes it was hard not to lose this faith. Some of the time, when nearly frozen to death, the words came out as: "*Why have you forsaken us?*"

Whether you were young or old, you could not, you must not, give up hope. We saw many people get through all types of illnesses without any medical help. They conditioned themselves to the fact that you could bend the mind over the body.

Not everyone survived. In the spring of 1941, Mrs Sliwinska, Aunt Krzysia's elderly mother, died. Mode of death: starvation. Reason of death: given up all hope. I have no idea how old she was, probably in her late-60s. At that age and in those circumstances, it was too easy to give up and hopefully go to a better place.

Christmas 1940 was the hardest time of all. The scene is set on Christmas Eve. There we are sitting in our miserable mud hut, the temperature outside around -40°C, inside around zero.

We are sitting on our suitcases and planks of wood. The roof, made of mud, cow muck, reeds and grass, is leaking. The floor being of hard soil is now muddy as well. We sit in our layers of sweaters, coats, even furs. It's cold, very cold. We huddle together for warmth. We cannot see the 'buran' or snowstorm outside; it has been snowing for weeks now. The hut is buried under the drifting snow. Our tunnel upwards is nearly blocked up. Soon someone has to go up its slippery 20 degree slope to unblock it, otherwise we will all suffocate.

So here we sit, the seven of us – Mother, Tota, Maciej, me, Aunt Krzysia, Ryszard and Mrs Sliwinska. In the middle of the circle is a battered suitcase, on which stands a stub of candle giving the only light. There is also a Holy picture of the Black Madonna and a jug of water, the residue of melted snow. We wish each other a 'better' Christmas, a Christmas sometime in the future and away from this prison. We think that perhaps Jesus was born in nicer surroundings. We have no Christmas Tree. There are no presents. My wish for a piece of bread does not materialise.

The food is a watery soup made from milled barley and thickened with flour. Just that, nothing else. It's our main course. But wait, what's this? A pudding? How did Mother manage to acquire tapioca and cocoa?

The meal being over, we all sit feeling terribly lonely, miserable and so far from everyone and everything dear to us. Depression descends. No-one says anything. A few tears are shed. We wonder how long we shall be able to exist like this. How many months until we will feel the warmth of the sun in the Spring? How many more Asian winters will we have to endure? Will we have enough possessions to barter with for food? What have we done to deserve this? The questions are asked endlessly but there is no-one who answers them.

All of a sudden the silence is broken. Mother sits up and breaks the despondent spell.

"Look at me, look at my eyes. We mustn't despair. We must be strong. Believe, you must believe! We will, we must get through this. Thankfully we are still together. We will remember this Christmas in many years' time as a nightmare. Others will not believe us. One day we will return to our beautiful home in Warszawa – to the warmth, security and happy days. Faith, we must have faith. God will protect us."

And so we huddled together, each one of us with our own memories; memories of happier times. Mine was of our last Christmas Eve in our Warszawa home at No1 Karwinska:

"It is Christmas Eve, 24th December 1938. Outside there is deep snow and the temperature is -10°C, inside it is a cosy 21°C. A happy electric atmosphere pervades the house. Mother wears a beautiful dark red dress, Father is in his best dark grey suit, and all of us children are smartly dressed. I am aged four, Tota fifteen and Maciej twelve. We are all excited and happy as a family. It is 5 o'clock and we are looking out of the large window to spot the first star to appear in the dark sky.

The large 'salon' is divided by large glass doors. Behind these we can see a huge Christmas tree decorated with brightly coloured baubles and festooned with ribbons. Many candles in their small holders have just been lit. The wonderful fragrance of the fir tree overpowers the air. Presents are piled under the tree – round ones, square, oblong and of every shape imaginable. At last Father says: 'There it is, the first star! Now let's go in'.

I rush in, Tota and Maciej follow with more decorum. I am at an age when I still believe in Father Christmas. I stop and stare and wonder what toys lie beneath the colourful wrappings, waiting to be opened. Our parents sit down demurely. As the youngest, I am expected to give out the presents. I get help from my sister to ensure that everyone is given presents in some kind of rotation.

I find a present with my name on it; it has an interesting shape, I wonder what it contains? Hastily unwrapping it, I know it's what I've always wanted; a remote control toy car. I am ecstatic and quickly forget about giving out any more presents.

It's now 6.30pm. Everyone has opened their presents and it is time to go and eat. The dining room has a big round table. There is the customary dry hay under the white damask table cloth (representing the stable in Bethlehem where Jesus was born). The silver cutlery is gleaming, the crystal glasses sparkling and at each place everyone has their own linen serviette beside the side plate. In the centre are two large lit candles; one white, one red, each in a silver candlestick. Before we sit down, we wish each other a happy Christmas and at the same time breaking each other's piece of unleavened bread.

We all sit down at the table. Christmas Eve is a non-meat fast day so there will be only fish eaten tonight.. Marynka is a wonderful cook. Benigna brings in all the food and places it in front of everyone. Michal helps with the wine. The first course is traditionally Polish Barszcz z uszkami – a clear beetroot soup like a consommé, with 'little ears' – pasta cases like ravioli stuffed with mushrooms. The next course is again traditional in Poland. A large eel in aspic, served in small moulds. This is then followed by another fish course which is the main course. It is kulebiak of carp, a favourite fish in Poland. The carp is baked in puff pastry and is delicious. The vegetable dishes are placed on the table for everyone to help themselves. These are croquettes and puree of potatoes, red cabbage and cauliflower with buttered breadcrumbs.

My parents drink Tokay, a popular rich red Hungarian wine. The dessert consists of compote of stewed fruit, an Austrian strudel and a poppy-seed cake.

Outside it is snowing. We can hear carol singers and go to the door to listen. Cakes are passed around to the singers and Father digs into his pocket for some zlotys to give them. We return inside. We are so happy. It is lovely and warm. Everything is perfection – or so it seems to me at my age."

It is time to return to our current harsh life. It's still winter and it never seems to end. January, February, March 1941. Would Spring ever come?

There were occasions during the latter part of that winter when an official from the Russian committee or some other administrator came to visit Tochka. We complained bitterly about our conditions but it was quite useless. The man either became suddenly deaf, said he could not understand us or plainly laughed in our faces. The only people who were at all friendly to us in Tochka were Kobash and Dzekir, both old Kozaks. These two would sometimes say a kind word or give some advice during all the disasters that plagued us in that sub-zero arctic weather.

During the whole of that winter, no post arrived; how could it? No-one could get through the frozen and snowed-up terrain. The whole area was lifeless; nothing moved. Even the wolves hid in their snow burrows, and if they howled, nobody heard them above the howling of the wind. How did we survive? It's beyond imagination, but survive we did - just.

We were never given permission to visit the nearest village except on one occasion. The occasion was some election and as usual we were commanded that we must vote, not that we could care less what the election was for. Mother and Aunt Krzysia were allowed, in fact ordered, to go to the village and vote. The journey remained in Mother's memory.

"There was as usual a Siberian frost with a bitter wind blowing. A Kozak told us to get onto a sleigh, driven by a pair of oxen. We travelled through a merciless snowstorm with the snow never ceasing all day. When we finally arrived at the destination, we looked like snowmen, just about frozen stiff. Friends who lived in that village were horrified at our appearance, not only the snow covered apparitions but what was under the snow. Thin, hollow cheeks, yellowish-grey faces and hands. We spent the night with these friends. This was the only time in that long winter when we were with friends who spoke the same language. The following day, both of us were ordered to return. Fortunately the weather on the trip back was reasonably calm, although horribly cold as usual."

In the Spring of 1941 there were disastrous floods. Seldom had there been such a fall of snow as in that particular winter. About the middle of April, the snows began to melt. The local Kozaks forecast that there would be floods. Our appeals to the manager of the 'firm' to be moved to a safer place were to no avail. The reply was: 'There is no danger, there will be no floods.'

As mentioned previously, near Tochka there was a deep gorge. In the summer, the river was only a trickle of water but that winter the gorge's river had swollen so much that the water was practically to the top of the gorge, and of course it was frozen solid. One day Maciej went to reconnoitre and returned saying that the ice had started to crack and move down the river. We soon surmised what was happening. The river became alive; the small, then the large icebergs bustled, pushed one against the other. The river level rose hour by hour as the melt continued, mainly due to the snow, now melted into streams, flowing from the steppes. In another day the really large icebergs had become alive, making a roaring and cracking sound. The ground shook each time they crashed against the sides of the gorge. Disaster was looming. A few days later the water reached the top of the gorge; it could not take any more water from the streams flowing in. Catastrophe! The river burst its banks. Suddenly the flat steppe changed in one day into an enormous lake. We watched all this desperate and filled with terror. The local Kozaks began to gather in the biggest of the cowsheds, carrying their belongings with them. This cowshed was on slightly higher ground than the rest.

On seeing the Kozaks' intention, we quickly decided we had to go there too if we were not to drown. By this time the 200 yards between our hut and the cowshed was already filling up. Somehow we waded in the ice cold water up to our knees, with me being transported on Maciej's back. We pulled our belongings behind us on a sleigh. There were of course mishaps on the way with Aunt Krzysia falling into the water and Ryszard more or less carrying her the rest of the way. Our belongings were soaked, but that was nothing new.

By the evening everyone assembled in the large cowshed. We settled down to await what would happen. Just before night descended, it was decided that everyone needed to get higher. The only way up was to climb to the roof inside the shed. The Kozaks had lifted planks of wood across the beams. So in the end we had to share accommodation. Thank goodness they had the heart to let us share this space.

All night we listened to the creaking, grating and jarring. It was a strange and frightening cacophony, enough to set the teeth on edge. Nobody slept. Silently we prayed, each in their own religion. It was a horrendous night, never to be forgotten. During the night there was a tremendous storm with torrential rain and lightning, a scene from a horror film. No, this was reality; our lives depended on a dam forming by the icebergs just off the river bank. If this dam cracked, we would be doomed as the icebergs surely would crush the cowshed like matchwood, as well as everything in its path. Our lives literally hung by a thread. Nobody knew what the morning would bring. As there were no windows to look out of, no-one knew what was going on outside.

At first light the Kozaks got down from the roof space. They ventured out to see how the land lay; well, not land, because it was all a big lake. They returned and predicted that the worst was over and the danger had passed. The icebergs held together during the night and had now slowly started to melt and flow in the river. By 10 am the sun began to shine, we started to get dry and the sun warmed our frozen bodies. By a miracle we had got through it.

Tochka looked in an awful mess. Neither the storm nor the melting, rushing water had damaged the huts. This was mainly due to the huts being still covered with a hard layer of compacted frozen snow and ice. However, with the warm sun came a quick thaw. The snow very rapidly turned to water that streamed into our hut through the long tunnel we had made. We went back as quickly as possible, again paddling through the freezing water. We had to rescue everything, hoping that the roof would not collapse. It took a whole day to take out the water in buckets and then the sodden mud had to be disposed of. The melting snow poured down on our heads through the thatch. With the water came the clay which had kept the thatch together. There was literally not a dry spot in the whole hut. Our priceless hay for sleeping got soaking wet. This was also used as kindling; no kindling meant no fire could be started.

Somehow we managed to get our hut into some kind of order. The few belongings which we had taken to the cowshed the previous day were brought back. Everything we possessed – which was minimal by now – was put out in the sun to dry. The sun shone all day; it was the first time we were warmed by the sun for months. In all our misery, we actually laughed out loud. Spring had arrived and we were still alive!

The roof could not be mended as the materials for it had not yet grown. So for a long time we slept under an old battered umbrella which probably had more holes in it than the roof. The roof leaked constantly. The one umbrella was over different heads each night. What a state of affairs. How did we manage not to fall ill with every type of illness you could possibly think of? How much more of this could we suffer? At least we were now not constantly in the dark. Most days the sun shone. We were warmer and we knew that the cruel winter was over – for that year anyway.

Our possessions dwindled rapidly. We could not even barter for any food now. We were in a desperate situation. Our footwear was in a terrible condition. Mother's lace-up shoes from Warszawa were already seven years old and the children's shoes were even worse. Although the shoes were mended continuously with pieces of untanned leather, they could not withstand the strain put on them in that climate and the work they were expected to perform.

The manager, having finally been moved by his conscience, at last gave us permission to move to the nearby larger 'firm'. Our spirits improved dramatically. Just the thought of leaving this indescribable hell-hole and moving to a new place was a great boost to our morale. The bonus included being with a larger group of people. Mostly they would still be Kozaks, but there would also be Polish families. On the negative side was a big problem. We would have to wait until the steppe dried up somewhat before attempting the journey.

A few days after the flood, the steppe still looked like a lake of water stretching to the horizon. There were some patches of grass here and there where the land was slightly elevated. The ground was so sodden that horses plunged up to their thighs in the soft clay.

The sun shone. Each day it seemed to get warmer. Our bodies enjoyed the warmth. There is nothing like warmth to bring back a positive attitude to life. Desperation and depression receded. Once again we were thankful to get through all our trials and hardships of the past four months of the Siberian winter and the horrendous floods. We were reasonably healthy and, apart from Ryszard's Babcia, Mrs Sliwinska, we were all still alive. If you added up all the problems – lack of food, lack of fuel at temperatures too cold to contemplate, wet and worn out clothes and footwear, living underground, the heavy physical and psychological strain and stress of just existing and keeping alive – it is a miracle and hard to believe that our health could stand it. Most probably the cold temperature must have had a bearing on keeping viruses and bacteria at bay most of the time. Mother said 'I cannot remember getting a cold at any time'.

There was now a lack of hay for the cows and there was no grass for them to eat. The result was they died of starvation, falling where they stood. Everyone got to the dead animals as soon as they keeled over. It was the Kozaks who of course had the best cuts. We were left to scavenge like hyenas for the rest. As we did not have fat for cooking, we had the suet. When a man is starving, he will eat anything at hand.

The day came when a decision was made that we would be able to travel across the steppe. The sun had done its work in drying the soil. It certainly gave new life to us. So it was that on 2nd May 1941 we finally left this accursed Tochka. Mother went to try and obtain permission to use a cart and oxen to carry our remaining possessions including the still valuable bed. Somehow Mother managed to persuade the Kozaks and hurried back to the rest of the family with the happy news. We loaded up all our meagre possessions with me sitting on the top trying to keep everything together. No-one looked back. We only had eyes to the front, to the future. Anything would be better. Surely it must be. The tide must turn sometime.

However, nothing went smoothly or to plan. One of the two oxen kept lying down in the mud. It needed superhuman strength to get it back on its feet and then needed much patience, as well as some Kozak swear words, to keep them moving. The cart got stuck in the mud, broken suitcases fell off the cart. Halfway to the Firm we exchanged the lazy ox for another beast that was feeding on the steppe. The journey continued at a quicker pace but even so it took us a couple of days to get there. The night was spent sleeping in the open under the stars.

We were glad to be back among a few Polish families who befriended us. It was so nice to be amongst our own people and solving problems became so much easier. Everyone helped us and we knew we were welcomed into their fold.

We were allocated a hut. As in Tochka, it did not come with 'all mod cons'; we had to repair, patch up, refit and generally make it fit to live in. It had two rooms, perhaps 'cells' is a more apt description. However, with two rooms we were definitely upsizing our accommodation. The roof once again was completely wrecked. Due to Maciej, Ryszard and Tota's work experience at Tochka, it did not take long to find the suitable materials. The work was completed within a day or two. The kitchen was useless but we could cook in the bread oven in the wall. So in no time at all the hut was made habitable and dry inside.

Maciej, Ryszard and Tota went to work. At first they worked as assistants to Russians in measuring land. Later they worked in the fields. As in the previous year, they worked in groups called 'Brigades'. They stayed out on the steppe for days at a time, sometimes for a stretch of a week or two. It was a dawn to dusk working day. They were given sufficient food, including plenty of bread. When they came 'home' they brought back some bread which they saved up. Mother, Krzysia and I did not work and consequently were not allowed any bread, so it was like manna from heaven when they returned for a day or two. Every worker had the right to buy food at government prices so Ryzsard and Tota were entitled to this, both being 18. As Maciej was only 15, he was considered under age and was not able to get this priceless work book. Nevertheless, Maciej had no option but to work.

"On 21st June 1941 the German army crossed the Russian border and the invasion of the vast country began under Hitler's Plan B which he called 'Operation Barbarossa'. This was the most extensive and the most savage of any modern military campaign. To begin with the Wehrmacht carried all before it. Within a matter of weeks, millions of Soviet prisoners had been taken. Wilno, Minsk and Kiev had been captured. They laid siege to Leningrad and by Christmas a Soviet collapse seemed imminent. The Wehrmacht pressed on towards Moscow.

All of a sudden Stalin needed help. The result was a Soviet-Polish Treaty signed on 30th July 1941 and a corresponding military agreement. In essence, the USSR agreed to annul the German-Soviet treaties of 1939, to restore diplomatic relations with the Polish Government in Exile in London and to permit the formation of an army drawn from the thousands of Polish soldiers being held as prisoners in Russia. The British were delighted – they now had two Eastern allies.

The military agreement followed on 14th August 1941. It stated that a new Polish army should be organised on Soviet soil. Later General Wladyslaw Anders, who had been a prisoner himself, was made its commander. 96000 men assembled. Anders had great difficulty with Soviet co-operation, both in armaments and feeding the men, eg he received only 44,000 rations for the 96000 men. In due course General Anders moved the troops from the Volga to Uzbekistan." [6]

---

[6] 'Rising '44' by Norman Davies

To get back to our modest hut at the Firm – we only heard the news about the German invasion a week after it happened. Remember we were in the middle of the steppe land of Kazakhstan and news took time to get there. Our first thought was that the road back to Poland was finally closed. The local population discussed the news with interest: *"The Germans would bring freedom for us. We will have a better life under the Nazis."* The news of the German advance and their victories did not reach us until it was a good week old. By this time the news was often exaggerated or completely false. The Polish group could not foretell what would happen to them. Somehow they knew there would be a change.

The bombshell news arrived not long after. The Russian-Polish pact had been signed. That was the first and last time that we heard from the Russian director of the Firm: *"Long live Poland. You are now free. We are your equals. It is forbidden for anyone to do you any harm or shout at you. All the same, you must work."*

From that moment, the attitude of the Russian officials towards us changed dramatically. They said that we must stay within the boundaries of the USSR but if we wanted we could find a better place to live. No-one actually knew where this 'better place' would be and how to get there. At least it gave a feeling of freedom, the long forgotten freedom, the freedom of which we had dreamed and prayed for. It had actually come true. We could hardly believe it. At last we could thank Hitler for something; we were no longer slave labour. We still imagined that by one way or another there might be a chance of returning to our country, back to our house, back to everybody and everything that we left two years ago.

These hopes were short-lived. They took away our Russian passports and gave us a kind of temporary certificate. We were told we must not go anywhere near the Russian-German front or to the larger towns. Nobody actually knew where the front was at any time, nor did they have much of an idea about the geography of this vast land. We certainly did not want to be caught by the German advance. All the Polish families discussed this for many a long hour. No-one came to any conclusion; we were all as ignorant as each other about the direction to take.

In the middle of August 1941, an NKVD top-ranking official by the name of Bogdansky came to confirm that we were at liberty to go anywhere we wanted. He advised Mother to go south to either Samarkand or Chimkent in Uzbekistan.

As usual there were many discussions and arguments among the Polish families about what to do and where to go. Some said it was safer to stay put – at least you knew the devil here rather than gambling on an unknown place. Some flatly refused to take on any risk; they tried to convince us to stay put. Mother made up her mind to go immediately. Surely life must be better than this somewhere, anywhere else. One of the advantages would be the warmer climate in the South.

I have found only one postcard written during our stay at the Firm and this was by my sister, Tota, on 18th May 1941. I notice that the postmark is very illegible and in Russian so it could even have been sent from Tochka just before we got to the Firm. Anyway it is the only card from this part of the world. The postcard is to a Sister M Catherina at 3609 N Redvale Ave, Chicago, Illinois, USA. Here I give the full message:

"It will be two years next month since I last saw you in Warszawa. How our paths have diverged. We are at opposite ends of the world. It is high summer with us at last. My brother and I work on the farms in order that we can exist. We often remember things we did then – so different from the present. The difference between heaven and hell. If it is at all possible to send us money, we would be delighted as life is very hard. Money can be received from America as many have had it. Life is so pleasant that I sometimes wonder why there is not an electric chair here. Not long ago my cousin Ryszard's grandmother died, Mrs A Sliwinska."

I must wonder how this postcard written to a Sister in Chicago found itself with the rest of the postcard collection. Strange..... I have no explanation.

CHAPTER 6

A BETTER DEAL - KARAKANDA

10TH SEPTEMBER 1941 – 1ST FEBRUARY 1942

On 10th September 1941 we finally departed from the Firm in Kazakhstan, having hired a Russian and his cart and oxen. We were still all together – Mother, Tota, Maciej, Aunt Krysia, Ryszard and myself. (Aunt Krysia's mother, Mrs Sliwinska, had died earlier that year.) As soon as we started on our journey, many other Polish families did the same. It took us two days to reach the last station on the railway line called Karagosly. It had only very recently been built, stretching into the steppe of Kazakhstan. It was so new that there was absolutely nothing around it; no houses, no shops, just the station – and that didn't even have an office.

It was good that we managed to bring some food and water with us. Nobody knew when there would be a train, typical for Russia at that time; one simply waited until a train came. As it was still summer weather, and therefore warm at night, we could sleep out in the open. Each family found their patch, cut down the dry grass and made a semblance of bedding themselves down. Our patch was about fifty feet from the railway track. At any time we had to be ready at a moment's notice to scramble aboard a train.

The train did not arrive that night, or the next day or the following one. We waited, all the time sleeping in the open, for a whole week. Thankfully there was no rain, but the nights were getting colder. We managed to bribe the railway officials at the station and in that way we got some water to drink and to wash in. Some is always better than none. Having now spent over 18 months living mostly without the 'luxury' of a daily wash, a few more days did not matter to us. If we smelled, so did everyone else. Anyway, the time was spent, as with any nomadic tribe, gossiping, playing paper games. In my case it was racing around and making myself a nuisance to everyone. There were no trees or bushes, so the 'conveniences' were some long grass a little way away from the family encampments.

No-one could believe it when we finally heard the train. Because the steppe was flat and stretched for hundreds of miles each way, you could not only hear the locomotive but see it a long way from the station. So it was that on 19th September we finally boarded the train with our, by now, depleted belongings. All the other Poles who had come to the station with us the previous week, piled onto the train as quickly as possible. Those of us who had worked at the 'Firm' received some money with which we could buy the tickets and of course the food for the journey.

Once on board, we actually got somewhere to sit which meant the five of us had to share two seats, sometimes three, and everyone took their turn. Being still quite small, I sat on someone's lap. The journey went on for ever. Each day we went further but stopping many times en route. It was certainly not a journey from A to Z; it was A to D, back to C, then change at G, stop in a siding, arrive at K, change to another train, go to T and after more stops, delays of one kind or another, side-tracked off the main line, back to T, then finally arriving at Z.

The journey in a crowded train with all sorts of Russians travelling, often with their goats or chickens, was not much fun. Most of the time sleep was impossible and we only managed it when the train had stopped somewhere en route. Our numerous bundles of possessions and packages of food had to be watched night and day. Our 'captured' seats had to be guarded constantly. It was pretty awful and very tiring. The journey lasted a whole month, mainly due to the Russian railway system. The 'timetable' was a joke; in reality it meant that if you wanted a particular train going in a certain direction, you had to wait for it to arrive. It could arrive in a couple of hours or a couple of days or even weeks.

It is hard to imagine the conditions in which the crowds would wait for a train. As you waited, you had to be in constant readiness to run for a seat or even a standing place, pushing with as much strength as possible. While doing this, you had to keep together as well as get all your possessions on to the train with you. There were times when we had to give up and therefore then had to wait for the next train.

We had a very general idea of the Russian geography – I do believe we had a school map of Russia, but certainly no details. The only way we knew we had to travel was south, so a compass would have been very useful. Somehow we managed quite well. By now everyone had a good knowledge of the Russian language. The trouble arose with changes of dialect or even language as we travelled through immense areas of the country.

A big problem while travelling like this was obtaining food. The train stopped at the bigger stations of Orenburg, Aktyobinsk, Aralsk and Iczyl-Orda for perhaps an hour, often it stopped nowhere near a station. At smaller stations such as Alga, Temir, Chelkar, and Yangi-Yer, it stopped sometimes for as little as a few minutes. At these stops someone had to get off to buy food, keeping a sharp eye on the train, otherwise he or she was liable to be left behind. Nine times out of ten it was either Maciej or Tota who got off and rushed to any vendors to buy the food and drink. The rest of us stayed behind guarding the seats and possessions. Quite often they just managed to jump back on as the train was already pulling away from the station. Mother was almost having a heart attack each time that happened. The usual diet was some unspecified soup with unknown ingredients but mainly cabbage called Shczy. The further south we travelled, the more we came across fruit, especially watermelons. These were a great delicacy to us as we hadn't seen fruit for a long time; they also quenched our thirst.

The stations were usually very clean and attractive. Many had plots with colourful flowers or small grass lawns.

During the whole of that month's journey, we did not manage to obtain one newspaper. We had no idea how the war was going, nor did we know much about the war in the whole of 1941, apart from hearsay or what we learnt from the NKVD officials at the Firm.

Some of the facts of this period of 1941: 6th April Germany finally invaded Greece. In the Middle East war raged with Romnel pummelling the Brits in the deserts, including sieging Tobruk for months until Montgomery managed to dislodge him on 9th December. The Italian Army surrendered in Abyssinia on 10th May.

On 15th October we finally arrived at our destination – the town of Chimkent in Uzbekistan. The railway station was large and had a refreshment room where, for the first time in a month we could eat actually sitting down at table - and we took a long time over it. The town seemed rich to us with many beautiful buildings. It certainly looked like we had arrived in a place 'of milk and honey'. We could buy as much bread as we wanted and there was an abundance of fresh fruit to choose from. Personally, I can still remember one particular fruit which I adored….apricots! They were fresh apricots and they tasted delicious. To this day I love apricots, both fresh and dried. There were also sweet melons, watermelons, grapes, figs, tomatoes and many others. After our starvation of the past 18 months, we ate all these delicacies with greed. This was food from heaven and our bodies needed it.

The Uzbeks were totally different from the Kozaks; they walked around clothed in rich colourful and beautiful national costumes. They were wealthy and cultured by comparison.

Unfortunately we could not find a place to stay in the town. In the end we all walked some way outside it and found a meadow with a big tree, which we thought would be ideal in the event of rain. The problem was that this charming and delightful site was across a small river. The river would be a security fence for us, or so we thought. We settled down quite comfortably to sleep as we were exhausted. Unfortunately at about 2 o'clock in the morning we were very rudely awakened by a great thunderstorm. The lightning and thunder was bad enough but torrential rain soon followed. The tree was not much use as an umbrella and the rain poured mercilessly, soon drenching us. We quickly realised that the little river was rapidly filling to become a fast-moving torrent. We had a moment of 'deja-vu' as we remembered our experience in Tochka when the river burst its banks. We definitely could not cross it until the rain stopped. Clutching as much of our possessions as possible, we managed to find a small hut further up the slope. This was a godsend and, in the relative warmth of the southern Autumn, we gradually dried out.

In the morning we went back to the town and found the office of the Russian 'important' officials. Of course we had to explain who we were and where we came from. Having shown them our certificates, which were duly stamped several times, we asked them for permission to be taken to some sovkhoz in the near vicinity of Chimkent. They seemed decent people and were delighted to help.

The officials lent us two big wagons and horses as transport. The six of us and two other Polish families left the town the following day. We did not know what to expect and this time hoped for a better deal. Please, not another Tochka. We travelled across very wild country without any sort of track. The Uzbeks driving the wagons seemed to know the area well. Our journey took us via undulating wooded country with some beautiful views but some of the slopes were very steep. On one of these slopes, one of the horses stumbled and fell. The passengers and luggage were thrown out. Fortunately, apart from the initial shock, nobody was hurt. The luggage, however, went tumbling down the slope and had to be retrieved bit by bit. At least the horse didn't suffer and we started off again.

The name of the Sovkhoz was Karakanda, a small Uzbek village with the huts situated on the top of a sloping valley. The view from the huts was quite magnificent when we arrived. It was probably the time of day; the sun was setting on the peaks of the Pamir Mountains. It could not look more different from the flatness of the steppes in Kazakhstan. I believe that Mother must have thought that her decision to come south had been a very wise one. The impression of all of us was that this was a very pleasant place.

The Uzbek officials of the sovkhoz arranged for all the new arrivals to be taken to the local school where we could bed down for the night. They gave us 'lepioshki' for the evening meal, a kind of noodle pasta which tasted like goats cheese. On the next day the head man assigned us to our living quarters. The hut we were to stay in had been used for storing wood. Although it was separate from the others, it was very dirty, the roof looked in poor shape and there were no windows. Mother decided, with the official's permission, to decline the one offered and instead we moved into a much better hut with another Polish family. These were the Chryns – a mother with her two daughters with whom we had travelled from the north.

We made ourselves reasonably comfortable, dividing the sleeping quarters in half. We all had hardly any possessions by now so there was enough room. As usual we scavenged for planks of wood for sleeping. A part of the hut was used for cooking using an old Uzbek stove. Here there was plenty of wood to gather for fuel – a great luxury for us.

Aunt Krzysia and Ryszard were sent to a neighbouring sovkhoz which was within walking distance. Often they used to come and join us so that we could all have a meal together.

The climate at the time that we stayed here – late autumn and part of winter – was not so cold. The Pamir mountains were covered with snow all the time. At Karakanda we did have snow but this was moderate in comparison to Tochka. The temperature varied from around 5°C to -10°C. We were kept reasonably warm in the hut by burning logs although, being wet, they would make a lot of smoke. We became pretty efficient at starting the fire – Tota was the expert!

Maciej and Tota worked in the fields gathering cotton. The whole of the valley below us was white with the balls of cotton on the dark bushes. They carried bags, slung over one shoulder, into which they put the manually harvested cotton. When filled, the bags were taken to a large cart. This would be repeated many times during the day but it was light work. After the picking was done, it was then sorted by hand, extracting any dried up leaves.

The Uzbeks had herds of cattle, goats and a type of sheep called Garacul; strange looking beasts with big curly horns. The cheese made from the sheep's milk was really delicious; we used it to provide flavour to our food.

Mother worked with the cattle. Her job was to keep them from eating the hay in the haystacks. This was not as easy as it sounds. In the winter the cattle used to get very hungry and they became very wily in finding ways to get to the hay. The hay was strictly rationed for them; there was never enough so the cattle got thinner and thinner and looked half starved, hence the rush to the hay stacks.

Soon Mother got to hear about a nearby gold mine. Actually this gold mine was rather primitive in the 20th century. If you turned back the clock to the Californian Gold Rush, then you would find here an identical way of sifting the gold from the stones and sand. The Uzbek men stood waist deep in the stream flowing down from the Pamir mountains; they had sieves or pans on long poles. These they held out into the running water collecting sand, stones and, if they were lucky, specks of gold. The Uzbek said that one day he would sell it if an opportunity arose.

Near these gold workings were the offices. You could take gold rings, brooches or in fact anything made of gold and in exchange receive coupons. The coupons could then be used to obtain the scarce and precious food for us. Mother still had some gold dollars – the same that were brought out of Poland stitched and hidden in her clothes. There were very few by now as most of them had already been bartered to buy food or had been stolen. With the precious coupons, we could buy sugar, rice and other necessary goods. Often the food we bought could then be exchanged with others for items such as eggs.

During the winter there was no fruit and no vegetables, so we were in the same situation as in the winter of 1940 in Kazakhstan. Lacking these nutritional foods meant of course a lack of vitamins. We all suffered badly from avitaminoza. I particularly suffered, covered with sores which became infected, my whole arms covered in pus. My sister went one day to the neighbouring Kolkhoz called Susjube, 23 miles away, hoping to get some kind of ointment. Being able to speak some Russian, if not the Uzbek language, she did manage to bring back something. Nobody was actually sure whether it was the right medicine, it probably was not as it did not seem to heal the sores; all it did was to sting me terribly. In the end, washing the boils with soap was the only way to help heal the sores.

Just after the New Year of 1942 Mother received a letter from the Polish Embassy in Kuybyshev advising her that there were Polish passports for us. She was told to send photographs to the Embassy. Mother went immediately with Maciej and Tota to Susjube to have their photos taken, although no-one knew whether there would be any photographic shops in the village. They were surprised to find several of them but not one of them had any film! Quite unbelievable but true. After all this was Uzbekistan, not Warszawa. They returned very depressed.

Life went on. When you compare it with Tochka, life here was luxurious. Nearby were some woods where Mother and I would go to gather the small branches and sticks for fuel. Sometimes Maciej used to borrow a small axe and chop down some bigger branches. This was actually forbidden but no one objected as long as it was done tactfully. Usually we had to cross streams and small rivers by wading across as there were no bridges. In the autumn you could jump from one stepping stone to another but in winter the streams and rivers were so swollen that the only way to get across was to cut one of the trees growing on the banks so that it fell across the river. Some of these 'tree bridges' were 25 feet above the river so everyone was always in a state of nervousness getting across. One day I did slip and fell into the icy water. Fortunately I managed to hang onto a branch of a small bush beside the stream. Maciej very valiantly climbed down to haul me out.

Around the 28th January we received an unexpected visit. A Polish soldier stood at our hut asking for Mother. He said his name was Private Nowak and told us that he had come from General Anders' Headquarters at Jangi-Jul. How he had found us is a mystery. We were overjoyed to see him and hear all his news. We of course did not know about all these soldiers formed into the army near the Caspian Sea in Turkmenistan. There was also a better surprise. He brought with him two large parcels from Father. Inside were warm clothes, shoes and food. What I remember most were the sweets, all wrapped in coloured papers. We had not seen sweets for two years. Seventy-five years on I can still see those 'delicacies'. When we gave some to the Uzbek children, they marvelled at them. Father also sent money which would soon be very useful to us.

We felt like we'd never had it so good! Everyone got into a party mood. We were overjoyed; we did not need any alcohol. We all put on our new clothes as if going to a party. How nice it was to get rid of the stinking old rags we had been wearing. And shoes, new shoes! Unbelievable - it was a day to remember.

Since Private Nowak was returning in two days' time, Mother decided to go with him to Susjube. Perhaps they would have the films this time. Then, after a family discussion, it was decided to ask the soldier whether he was willing to take us with him. Probably he was rather taken aback. After some thought he agreed, but did we know all the problems? Firstly we were not supposed to leave Karakanda without official permission. Secondly, how were we to get to the railway station with our possessions? Thirdly, it was a long way by rail and we needed enough money to buy the tickets. Also, there was Aunt Krzysia and Ryszard to think of.

We decided that we probably would not get permission to leave and so we would have to do 'a midnight flit'. Mother knew a certain Uzbek who was greedy for money. She went to see him and he promised to let us borrow a small two wheeled cart and a horse. A great deal of money was given in exchange.

In three days we packed everything we possessed onto this cart. Maciej went to the next sovkhoz to tell Aunt Krysia and Ryszard our plan and to ask them to meet us early the next morning at a certain place on our way to the station at Susjube. Maciej returned to say that Ryszard was not feeling well but that they would meet us as planned.

CHAPTER 7

TO ENGLAND BY LAND, SEA AND DESERT

1ST FEBRUARY – 25TH SEPTEMBER 1942

It was in the first week of February 1942 that we left Karakanda. It was 6am, still dark, frosty and very cold. I was lifted onto the cart along with all the bundles of luggage. The other four, including the soldier, pushed the cart and at the same time encouraged the horse by pulling, much shouting and giving it a good prod from behind. The terrain was of course the same as that which we had travelled across in October. Up and down the slopes of the hills we pushed and pulled.

When we reached the agreed meeting place, there was no sign of Kryzsia and Ryszard. Had they not understood where we were to meet? It was now starting to get light. Maciej was despatched to their village to see what had happened to them.

As we were waiting, an Uzbek came galloping up on horseback and ordered us to return. Obviously the commotion of our exit had woken a few and they had told the officials. Although it was difficult to understand the Uzbek language, we understood well enough that we were being told to explain why and where we were going as we had no legal permission to leave the sovkhoz.

Private Nowak had a bright idea: *"As I am in uniform, it will seem as if I have authority and that is always something that these people take notice of. I will go with their men back to the village and sort something out."* Fortunately, when he returned to Karakanda, the so-called 'procurator' was there. This man spoke Russian. Nowak told him that he had been sent from the Polish HQ and ordered to bring the wife of a general and his family back with him. He must have made a good impression for this Uzbek only asked him to sign some kind of papers and gave permission for us to leave.

When Nowak returned to us, Mother said she would recommend him to General Anders and told him he should receive a medal for his bravery. Meanwhile Maciej had come back with the news that the other two could not join us as Ryszard had flu and was therefore not in a fit state to travel. They hoped somehow to follow us later.

At this point, I must mention that although there must have been correspondence relating to this time, especially between Father in the UK and Mother in Uzbekistan, none seems to have been kept.

On reaching Sasjube, Private Nowak took us to see a representative of the Polish Army in Russia. He not only fed us but also gave up his bed for Mother. The rest of us bedded down in another room. Naturally we had to wait a couple of days for a train. During this time Nowak found a Russian airmen's canteen and asked them for bread and some kind of a meal. They not only invited us in but we were shown to a table, properly laid for lunch, and were served an excellent meal. Miracles do happen occasionally, even in those harsh times in Russia. Before leaving, we were given two loaves of bread to take away with us. We would soon be leaving Uzbekistan – not exactly an enchanted land, but certainly warmer.

We were now faced with the problem of getting tickets for the train. Not an easy matter as we only had a limited amount of money. Nowak somehow managed to get four tickets – it wasn't just a case of having enough money, tickets were allocated on an 'importance' scale. Your rating on the scale depended on whether you were Russian/Uzbek, whether you were in the army (Russian preferably) and whether you could give a good bribe to the ticket collector. Three days later we managed to squash into the already packed train going to Tashkent.

As was usual on these trains in Russia, the seating was benches either of wood only or occasionally with some soft padding. The bonus was that there was plenty of room underneath for luggage or for yours truly to hide under. Although we only had four tickets, there were actually six of us – Mother, we three children, Private Nowak and one other young man who was going to join the Polish Army. So each time the ticket collector came through to check the tickets, I had to get under a bench where I was hidden by luggage while one of the men would either hide amongst the suitcases on the luggage rack or disappear to the lavatory.

We arrived safely in Tashkent after a journey of about 6 days. Being a large town, the station also had a dining room where we managed to obtain a bowl of soup and a hunk of bread each. Nothing is near perfect in these places. There was a shortage of spoons; in fact we could not find any at all. There were knives and forks aplenty but no spoons. Seated at our table was an old Russian comrade. This character was dressed in the filthiest clothes imaginable, unshaven and smelt to high heaven. However, he did have a spoon! On finishing his soup, he licked his spoon dry. He looked over at us and, seeing we had none, said *"Now that I have finished, take mine to eat your soup."* It did not even occur to us to refuse this bit of goodwill. On the contrary, we were delighted to obtain this necessary 'tool' to eat our soup, each one of us taking turns.

We went out into Tashkent, walking along the streets, admiring the cleanliness and width of them. We admired the beautiful minarets, mosques and palaces decorated with incredible ceramic ornamentation. We came across a very noisy and colourful oriental bazaar selling everything from samovars (a large and ornate Russian tea urn heated by a built-in charcoal burner) to copper implements, things made from silver, oriental carpets and much more.

Having waited another day, we took another train to Samarkand. Once again we managed to buy some food to sustain us. In this town there were many architectural monuments and colourful markets where we could buy fresh fruit to eat.

The cities of Samarkand and Bukhara, among others, were located at the mid-point of the Great Silk Road in Asia; the road travelled by Alexander the Great and Genghis Khan. It is fascinating to think that these cities were the mid-points of trade between China and Europe many centuries ago.

We then managed to find a train that would hopefully take us through Turkmenistan to the Polish Army Headquarters. The whole journey from Karaganda to Jangi-Jul took us about 12 days. No doubt there were a lot of mishaps on the way but I do not have any further information of that time, only to say we six arrived safely, travelling all the way using the four train tickets.

So it was that we arrived in Jangi-Jul on about 16th February 1942. At this stage soldiers were still arriving from all parts of Russia where they had been imprisoned as POWs. They had all been captured by the Russians in September 1939 and stayed in various prisons and labour camps until Poland became an ally of Russia after Germany's invasion of Russia on 21st June 1942. As already mentioned in a previous chapter, a Soviet-Polish Treaty was agreed on 30th July 1941, within which a stipulation was made to form a Polish Army on Russian soil, with General Anders as Commander. Young men who, similar to ourselves, had been deported with their families and were now old enough to join the army, congregated here as well.

We were now back with our countrymen and over the worst period of our lives. Mother's memory of the initial reception was as follows:

"When I went to register our names with the Polish official at the camp to say we had arrived, he said rather sharply that he did not really know why we had come here as it was a military camp. It was most unpleasant to hear such a negative response. After all our journeys, trials, tears and hunger, I expected something better."

However, it did not take long for Mother to find General Anders. He was kindness itself and greeted her cordially. The last time Mother had seen him was when he was in the POW train in Przemysl in December 1939. He allowed us to live within the camp and later organised for our passports to be brought over from Kuybishev.

Our quarters were in a big hut. We were not alone though; with us were six other Polish families who had arrived at the camp from different parts of Asia in similarly strange and unusual ways. Each family had one large mattress on the floor. Those first few days were pleasant enough; each family had their own stories to tell. Everyone looked thin, under-nourished and with greyish unhealthy complexions. Time was spent ruminating about past experiences and wondering what the future would bring. Friends were made; friends we were to travel with on the next part of the journey.

More and more soldiers were arriving. The camp did not have enough accommodation. As it was, all the soldiers were sleeping in tents anyway. On our fifth day in the hut, General Anders gave orders that all families must move out of the camp and into the nearest town as the quarters were needed for arriving soldiers and any officers. Mother managed to get special attention (she was good at that) from General Anders. He promised her that he would get someone to find us a place in the town. The other families moved out but we stayed put, awaiting the promised lodgings. Since they could find no room in the town, they gave us a separate room still in the camp grounds. This was lovely and private and we were hoping that we would be left alone.

Unfortunately, after three days, our privacy was invaded. A great storm, followed by torrential rain, flooded the tents of the Women's Volunteer Service and they all had to move into our room for shelter. The next day we were moved again. This time it was into a shell-type hut where we were given three beds and we stayed here for the next four weeks.

We were delighted to receive another two parcels from Father. In the parcels were more clothes and shoes. We now had shelter, some decent clothing including coats and shoes – we were beginning to feel like human beings again. We used to eat in the soldiers' canteen. The food was good and we could obtain butter, cheese and dried apricots in the town. Our bodies were gaining flesh and a more healthy appearance. We were, in all senses, coming back to life!

There was still no sign of Aunt Krzysia and Ryszard so Mother sent a telegram to them. How they actually received it, I wonder to this day, but they did receive it and very fortunately they arrived at the camp only two days before we sailed.

I will now give some information about my uncle, aunt and cousin.

My aunt Krystyna or Krzysia (diminutive name, very often used in Poland) had an extra responsibility in not only having a son, Ryszard or Rys, with her in Asia but also an elderly mother, Mrs Sliwinska, who died of starvation in the Spring of 1941. Krzysia's husband was Colonel Wlodzimierz or Wlodziu, who, it has been mentioned, arrived with the Polish forces in France in 1940, then escaped to Switzerland before France capitulated and was interned there (probably for the rest of the war). Krzysia and Ryszard travelled with us in Asia and to Persia and Palestine. I am unsure as to whether Aunt Krzysia travelled with us for the rest of the journey back to England. She did arrive in England at some time in the early 1940s, as did her husband. When my uncle was demobbed in 1947, they bought a house in Balham, London. They both died there in the 1980s.

Ryszard joined the Polish army at the age of 17 when he got to Jangi-Jul (where a Polish army was being gathered from newly freed soldiers who had been imprisoned by the Russians). He went with them via Persia to Palestine. The rag-tag army from Russia became the Polish 2nd Corps that was later to fight in the Italian Campaign of 1944/5 and become famous for capturing Monte Cassino after many months of fighting alongside British, Canadian and other Commonwealth countries. He was posted to Scotland where he gained a commission. He then joined the Polish 1st Armoured Division which landed in Normandy in 1944. As part of the Canadian 1st Army, the Polish Division fought in the Low Countries, including 'closing of the Falaise Gap' as it was known on 21st August 1944. They advanced through part of France, culminating in the capture of the German Naval Base at Wilhemshaven in May 1945. His final rank was Cavalry Captain.

I remember Ryszard well, especially in my early years in London. Firstly, seeing him in his uniform in 1943, then later when he often used to visit us. He was always a happy go lucky type, laughing and joking and a great character with the girls.

My best memory of him was in August 1956. After finishing the 3 year Hotel Management Course at Battersea College of Technology, three of us went hitch-hiking through France and Spain. To cut the story short, I was left penniless or, rather, franc-less after losing my two companions who had not only my money but also my passport. I got to Paris, walked into the Polish club there to get help and who do I bump into? Ryszard, plus a friend, with whom I then stayed for a week. Ryszard took me around the sights such as the Louvre and Versailles as well as the Moulin Rouge. By the end of the week I had received back both money and passport by post.

On 20th July 1957, I was Ryszard's best man, 'sporting' a hired wedding suit of top hat and tails. He was in his officer's uniform. The whole ceremony was held in Brompton Oratory, London. He married Wanda Raczynska, eldest daughter of Count Edward Raczynski, the Polish Ambassador to the Court of St James' in 1939, later becoming the Polish President in Exile. After the fall of communism, the confiscated Raczynski estate in Rogalin, near Poznan, with its baroque palace and magnificent parkland, was returned to the family. They immediately gave it to the nation, with the proviso that Wanda could keep a small apartment for herself.

After he was demobbed in 1947, Ryszard worked in insurance. From the 1960s he worked at the Polish Institute and Sikorski Museum in London, researching and preserving the history of Polish forces, especially those in WW2. He was elected its chairman in 1979. He died on 29th June 2008, aged 84.

In August 2008, Maciej, Kasia (Maciej's second wife) and I visited Rogalin. There we met Wanda who showed us around the enormous palace which, at that time, was being completely renovated. We visited the Raczynski Mausoleum underneath the Chapel where Ryszard and all the Raczynskis are buried.

To go back to my Mother's account, now we were back to six again but, as mentioned above, Ryszard stayed behind. General Anders instructed us to board the first ship that sailed. So, on 28th March 1942 the first train containing both soldiers and civilians set off from

Jangi-Jul to the port of Krasnovodsk on the Caspian Sea. We were the first of thousands, including 40,000 orphans who somehow managed to cheat exhaustion, starvation, disease or death to get out of this accursed land to freedom. There were many who never got this far and perished on the Asian steppes and in the gulags of Siberia.

After our arrival at this port station, we were all taken to a big square in the town. We were told to give up all our Russian passes and then to walk with our bundles to the port before embarkation. On the quay we waited all together, as did all the family groups. The scene around us was awful; everyone in their old torn and disintegrating clothes, looking about 20 years older than they really were; the children crying, those that had mothers trying to console them; some old men stumbling, chatting, whispering to each other, some solemn, trying to forget their experiences and hardships of the last two years. Mostly they looked thankful that their ordeal was over -it was a picture of people, from the very young to the very old, who had been shut out of the civilised world; they had been humiliated, treated worse than animals, their minds tortured, their bodies small, bent, ill and their eyes lifeless. Near us was a group of orphans; one girl was lying on a made-up stretcher, too weak to walk. She did not manage to last out and died 15 minutes before embarkation. On another side was a bigger group of orphans looking sad, some crying, filthy in their rags, some without proper shoes, others without any warm clothes or coats; half starved, they shivered in the cold. I remember seeing a group of older women with their children, openly crying, but it was the kind of crying that said, "Thank you Jesus, thank you Mary for saving us".

It was a melancholic and agonising scene, a scene of dramatic proportions, reflecting the horrors, the hate, the fear left behind and the hopes, expectations and the promise of the future.

Everyone got very excited when it was time to embark. An NKVD official read out the list of names. Everyone feared that his name might be left out. At last our names were called. We picked up our belongings and boarded the ship. As our feet touched the deck, we knew that our exile in Soviet Russia had ended for good. As the ship started to sail, everyone started to sing the Polish anthem:

"*Jeszcze Polska nie Zginela, Poki my Zyjemy*" (Poland will never fall, whilst we are alive) – a very moving finale. Everyone was laughing and hugging each other. The decks were crammed with the soldiers and civilians. There was hardly any room to move but nobody complained.

After about three days in this old rusty ship, which probably was first seen on water forty years ago, at last we saw land – Persia, later to be called Iran. We disembarked at a port on the Persian peninsula and a convoy of lorries took us to a camp. We were to spend a few days under canvas in tents. Everyone was disinfected, deloused and generally made human again by general cleaning. Having received our clothes by parcel from England, we were now most presentable and looked out of place among the rest. Mostly the others' clothes were discarded, the Red Cross providing second hand but clean clothes in exchange. Among the ladies who were organising the camp was a Countess Potocka, a well-known aristocrat from Poland and known to Mother of course.

Our connections and the intervention of the Countess meant that we were soon transported to Tehran and, for the first time for two and a half years, stayed in luxury at the Danish Embassy. I have no idea why the Danes gave us this hospitality. My Father's name and rank must have been worth something in those days! Anyhow it was a treat and a pleasure to soak in a bath, sleep in a bed with clean, crisp white sheets, walk on carpeted floors, sit at a table, beautifully laid with cutlery, eating sumptuous food and drinking from sparkling crystal glasses. It all felt very strange and I for one found it difficult to get accustomed to this type of living. We all needed some acclimatisation. I disgraced myself, sitting down on the bidet to do my business instead of using the toilet. Well, how was I to know? I had never seen one of those before!

We spent about a month in this very comfortable accommodation. It was like living in a hotel. During the day we visited the city, rich in architecture and beautiful gardens. The Shah was like an emperor – he would still be on his throne up to the 1980s. *(In June 1976 on the way back from my teaching post in Fiji (1974-6), the Air France plane carrying us back to the UK landed in Tehran. We spent one night there before we caught our connecting plane and went to see the Shah's jewels and other glittering gold and silver treasures).*

I am guessing at the dates during this period but the five of us must have left about 4th April 1942, together with the Polish Army. Many army lorries formed a convoy and we travelled with them. General Anders wanted to move his whole army as quickly as possible to the Middle East. There they would be able to join the British Army and fight against Rommel in Egypt and Libya.

This part of our journey was probably very interesting. Unfortunately I personally have very little recollection of it. From Tehran to Palestine (now Israel) it must have been over 1000 miles by road. The scenery must have been spectacular, especially in Persia where we would have had to cross 6-9,000 ft mountains. I do remember stopping in Baghdad in Iraq. As it was anything but a tourist stop, I don't believe we saw much of it.

Each evening the convoy stopped. Food and water was dispensed and we slept in tents within the main army encampment. Songs were heard, harmonicas produced, Polish folk dancing by lit fires. It was good to be amongst our own people. An early start was made, especially once we were driving through the Syrian desert in Arabia. I do remember that we were ordered not to drink water during the day, only in the morning and when we stopped at night. I also have memories of the dry stifling heat all day and then the really cold nights.

We must have crossed the Euphrates and Tigris rivers and perhaps were in between the two rivers, known as Mesopotamia. The desert stretched for hundreds of miles. I did see mirages of villages and running water. Most of the time we crouched low with clothes wrapped around our faces to protect us against the sand getting into our mouths and noses. Everything became gritty. The sand got everywhere. There were times when the lorries had to be dug out of the dunes. Everyone hoped that the drivers knew where they were going. It was a very monotonous journey through the desert where nothing seemed to live, even exist. The water was rationed and the food in the evenings was gritty but we did at least eat.

Having now travelled through Jordan, we arrived in Palestine. I have an actual date of arrival as this was noted in Tota's diary as 9th May 1942. Together with our army soldiers, we de-camped at Rehovith camp.

During the twelve days that we stayed in the camp, many friends were made, many stories told of the horrible existences of us all. They shared their accounts with us which would have been similar to those recounted in the book 'Keeping the Faith': [7]

"10th February 1940 – in the morning about six or seven o'clock. A bang on the door. The militia walked in and they said to father, 'Hands up, stand in the corner'. They said to mother, 'You pack what you can manage, but don't pack much because you have to walk to the railway station'. So you can imagine, what could we take? Mother put a lot of clothes on us. We could hardly walk... It was such a severe winter and there was a long, long train for taking cows. They weren't for humans and they packed us in. There were about fifty in one carriage, can you imagine? They locked the door, the windows were covered with white ice. We couldn't see anything but I could hear whispers of our neighbours and aunts and uncles."

Then there was a woman who imparted a similar version:

"We were herded into cattle wagons for transportation. The trucks were dark and locked. There was only one small window at the top. 'Bunks' had been made – planks of wood on the side of the wagon. Cramming in as many individuals as they could, we stood during the day and slept of a fashion at night. We were given no food at all for the final two days. We were expected to eat anything we had brought with us. People were distressed and crying. One woman gave birth to a

---

[7] 'Keeping the Faith' by Tim Smith and Michelle Winslow

stillborn child. The guard threw the body off the train when we reached a station. You had to try not to touch the wooden walls when you slept. Your hair would stick to the wood because of the ice and break off. It was bitterly cold."

A woman who was a school teacher informed us of her job in Asia:

"I worked for about two months on the steppes with a Kazak family. I was the only European there. I had a baby with me. We had just one big kettle for everything. I used to cook in it, bathed the baby in it, washed the nappies in it and everything else in it."

A man who was a postmaster before the war commented on the lack of food:

"The only kind of meat we got was when a horse died and had to be destroyed. I was working with a horse. We used to drag trunks from the forest to the saw-mills. We were short of vitamins and everything. A lot of people were losing their sight at evening time. Even when it was light, you could only see like you were in a fog. We used to follow the horses – they took us back to the place where we were living."

A young soldier, one amongst hundreds who must have said the same words:

"Germany invaded Russia and we didn't know what was going on. They told us to gather – Polish men only. They told us 'You are free people because we want you to help us to fight the Germans.'"

One of his friends added:

"It was Churchill who made the agreement with Stalin that the Poles will be amnestied. We were furious about it. What amnesty? We didn't commit any crime."

A third soldier had his say:

"General Anders was like Moses to us because he led us from Russia into the free world."

There was an aristocratic lady by the name of Wanda Zaleska who spoke up:

"We started to travel, but we had no food, and if you had no food, you would die during the journey. There was no way to survive because they didn't give you even a piece of bread. What dreadful conditions, dreadful. People falling down and nobody cared, because of hunger. And then there was typhoid, dysentery. You've never seen anything like it. People were dying like flies. Travelling by train there was no water, so we managed to put a string on a little bucket to catch snow. We walked on dead people, believe me."

And then the daughter talking about the death of her father on a train to Uzbekistan:

"In a town where the train stopped, my father and myself went out to try to buy something. We still had some gold, a few things, mama's necklace and clock. So of course you could sell it and buy something from the Uzbeks. Father managed to buy soup to bring to the transport that was waiting for us but my father dropped it. He had a severe heart attack. People behind us ran quickly. 'What's happened?' they called. The militia was summoned. They said 'He's dead. If you want to see where your father's going to be taken you can go with us'. They took us in a little car and we came to a huge building. As they opened the gate, all I could see were bodies of dead people. They just took my father's arms and legs and swung him right to the top of the pile. They shut the gate and that was all."

Here is an expression of the horrors of so-called life in Soviet Russia:

"In Uzbekistan there was a place where they were collecting soldiers so Stan, my brother, went to the army and I stayed in a little village. Huts were made of clay, a bit of straw, and lice. We found a lady; she was so badly bitten by lice and everything, she wasn't able to help herself. She must have had TB and in three or four days she died. We had to report it and they came and took the body away. We checked everything out because we were afraid of lice. If they bit you, you might catch typhoid. They cut all our hair off and took our clothes because of the lice. About six weeks later we left for Iran."

An old man now describes their arrival in Persia:

"When we got to Iran, there were thousands of tents on the sand, near the Caspian Sea. This is where they kept us. Of course, they took everything off us again. They shaved and washed us to stop epidemics. They gave us some food but we had to be very careful because we were so hungry. A lot of people died because they didn't have food for a long time and they started eating, grabbing everything, and they had problems with their insides and died. You had to be very careful, eat small portions, avoid heavy things, and those who took no notice wouldn't survive. Even drinking water – just a sip and stop, then an hour later try again."

Now, back to our family itinerary……

On 23rd May 1942, our family moved out of the camp. Our Father had connections with the Polish Army officers in Palestine, and through them we managed to find housing in a flat in Telaviv. Looking back to Tota's diary of 1939, I notice addresses of Polish Forces in the Middle East and in particular in Telaviv. Often there is an address noted, even how to find the flat, ie 'entrance from Hayerken'. There is even our address noted as Hagalili 23. Unfortunately my sister does not say how long we were there, but by my reckoning it must have been a couple of months.

My memories of Telaviv were of going to the lovely sandy beach, of having to wear a pith helmet thing against the strong sun, and of houses all painted white. Mother was invited to parties at the Polish officers' club and of course to the many Poles who had come up via Tehran. It was a time of good food – meat, vegetables and fruit. To this day I remember seeing a huge lorry filled to the rim with beautiful oranges just harvested. I still have a forage-cap, a small size one for a seven year old boy with a metallic Polish eagle pinned to the top. It must have been given to me by one of the soldiers.

Palestine in 1942 was under British administration; the British still aimed to keep Palestine as a predominantly Arab country after the war.[8]

No correspondence was kept from either Persia or Palestine, apart from an Airmail letter cover from Father to Mother, postmarked London 28th June 1942. It was addressed to Polish Forces, ME222 (which was Middle East Forces in Palestine). It was passed by British Censor. It was not received by Mother – there is a note on the envelope in Polish 'Departed to England'. The letter was redirected to "Town Major, London" – whoever that could be I wonder? Then this invisible man redirected the envelope to 53, New Cavendish. It was then redirected again to Father who was living in the flat in Chalk Farm, with the address 91 Eton Hall, Eton College Road, London NW3 and arrived there at last on 23rd November 1942, returned five months after it was sent. When arriving back in England in September 1942, all the family joined Father at this address.

We left Telaviv on about 10th July 1942, travelling by train to Port Said (now known as Bur Sa'id) in Egypt. We were taken to the port by someone from the Diplomatic Corps and saw the ship that was moored – we were to travel on nothing less than the RMS Queen Elizabeth I (see p165). Being only a few days till my 8th birthday, I was not very tall and I still remember when I looked at this ship, I thought of it as a giant with its five decks and two huge funnels; the whole structure looked enormous.

Here is the interesting story of this beautiful ship. It was owned by the Cunard Line and launched on 27th September 1938. Due to the War in Europe, her maiden voyage ended on 7th March 1940 with a surprise arrival in New York Harbour. She began this voyage by secretly leaving her fitting-out basin and heading for her home port of Southampton. As she headed down the Clyde, her captain opened his orders, which directed him to take his new charge to New York.

On 21st March 1940, further orders were received to proceed to Singapore and then Sydney to meet her future running mate, RMS

---

[8] 'Rising '44' by Norman Davis

Queen Mary. After conversion work was completed, she spent the remainder of the war moving troops around the world. On most voyages she carried between 13,000 and 15,000 troops. During WW2 service she carried over 811,000 passengers and sailed over 500,000 miles. At 83,637 gross registered tons, she would be the largest passenger ship afloat for the next 34 years. She had a speed of 30 knots and therefore could outrun any submarine.

She was released from war duty in March 1946 and underwent an extensive refit. She finally left on her maiden passenger voyage in October of the same year and began a 20 year career of transatlantic crossings. During the mid to late 1960s, as the number of people crossing the Atlantic by ship continued to decline, Cunard began offering her for more cruises. Unfortunately she lacked many of the essentials expected of a cruise ship and even the addition of a swimming pool and central air conditioning in 1965 proved too little, too late and the once great ship continued to lose money.

My personal memory of the ten days that we sailed on this great ship is clouded due to my young age at that time and the seventy years' time shift. So what has stuck in my brain cells? The ship was crammed with Italian prisoners of war, captured in the Middle East. Evidently we were given preferential treatment with an excellent cabin and meals with the officers. The captain even took all of us on a tour of the vessel, including down to the bowels of the ship. This was a complete surprise to us; right down below was a farm! When I tell this to people now, they do not believe me. There were cows, sheep, chickens and pigs. Yes – and a slaughter house. Just imagine the chef ordering so many chickens to be killed for the day's menu. I presume refrigeration was in its infancy in those days.

There are two other things that seem to have stuck in my mind. Number one was a horrendous storm. Everyone was sick as a dog and, as we went to the top deck to get some fresh air, we certainly got that and saw the waves crashing right over the top deck. Number two was when there was an alert, when they thought they saw a German submarine. Fortunately it was a false alarm, but everyone had to get to their station by a certain boat.

The QE1 sailed all the way to England – the long way round via the Cape of Good Hope. Of course at this time the Mediterranean was crawling with German subs, naval vessels and planes. In the Indian Ocean it could outrun any submarine as it had phenomenal speed.

So our 10 days aboard began at Port Said, then through the Suez Canal, passing Ismailia to Suez itself. Then the ship sailed via the Red Sea, Gulf of Aden and into the Indian Ocean. Keeping near land, we must have passed Somalia, Kenya, Zanzibar, Mozambique and finally the long coast of South Africa, arriving in Cape Town on about 20th July 1942. I presume we docked at Port Elizabeth and I remember we were met by someone from the Polish Consulate. This individual helped himself to linen – sheets and towels – as souvenirs of the ship! He took us by car to the Queens Hotel at Sea Point in Cape Town. I still have notepaper and a letter card with a picture of the hotel with Lion's Head in the background (meaning the Table Top Mountain) of Cape Town. The hotel looks very luxurious.

What do I remember about our sojourn in Cape Town? The answer is – not very much. We must have spent about six weeks here. I was now just past my 8th birthday and I still had not been to any school. Mother decided that I had better start. I have a receipted bill from the Loreto Convent, Sea Point. It says that one guinea was paid for Term III (18th August – 18th September). I do know that I never attended a whole month in this school. In fact I ran away after the first day; no matter how much persuasion was put my way, I was not going anywhere near this school any more. The one guinea paid must have been for the one day's attendance! The 'with thanks' receipt is over a South African Penny stamp dated 18.08.42.

The only other thing I recall is being taken to the beach. It was cold, very blustery and rocky.

As far as correspondence is concerned, there is one Registered letter envelope with 5½d British stamps sent by Father from London N4. It is addressed to Mrs Maria Dembinska, Polish Consulate General, 227 Boston House, Strand Str, Cape Town, S.Africa. Although someone at the London W4 Post Office was slap happy in applying not one but four

'Registered' postmarks on the back of the envelope, there is no indication of a date that it was posted. However, it must have taken a long time to arrive as there is a receiving mark of the Polish Consulate dated 29th September 1942. It was then returned to the sender's address as on the back of the envelope – 2 Bryanston Court, George St, London W1 (at the time this was the Polish President's offices in London). From there it got passed on to 91, Eton Hall, Eton College Rd, NW3 London (where Father lived). I wonder when it actually came back because we had already arrived in Britain on 25th September 1942.

On approximately 8th September 1942 we left Cape Town on the P&O liner Stratheden (see p165).

Stratheden was built by Vickers-Armstrong at Barrow-in-Furness, launched on 10th June 1938 and her maiden voyage to Australia started on 24th December 1938. To give her specifications, she was 23,722 tons, length 664 ft x beam 82ft, with one funnel, twin screw and a speed of 20 knots. The accommodation was for 448 first class and 563 tourist class passengers. To compare it to QE1, the Stratheden was approximately 8½ times smaller. Between 1939-1945, she also served as a troopship. She was reconditioned in 1946-47 and resumed her P&O Line service in June 1947 until 1964. Having been sold and renamed a couple of times, she was finally scrapped at Spezia in 1969.

Our voyage must certainly have taken over two weeks. Once again I believe we had POWs with us, but my brain is completely defunct as to recollecting anything except for stopping perhaps for refuelling at Freetown, Sierra Leone.

So we finally made it to Britain, arriving in Liverpool on 25th September 1942. You can imagine the joyous reunion with Father, who was at the dock to meet us. It was almost exactly three years since we had last seen him.

CHAPTER 8

THE FAMILY IN LONDON

1942 - 1945

The family, now all five of us, arrived at Kings Cross Station on a train from Liverpool. We had made it to London, England. It was the evening of 25th September 1942.

As usual by now, everything was strange for us. We knew very few words of the language, but surely we should have been used to arriving in a foreign land. After all, we had travelled through so many different countries, each with its own speech and local dialect. There was Russian, Kazak, Uzbek, Persian, Arabic, Egyptian and English on our travels.

Father had already been in England for well over two years, having arrived here via Hungary, France and Scotland. Although he had learnt English, it was very basic. Most of his time up till now was spent with the Polish Forces and therefore he did not have to use English as a language.

At the station we all piled into a taxi together with our minimal luggage. As it was already dark, we didn't see much of the city and shortly arrived at the enormous block of flats of Eton Hall. There must have been about a hundred flats in this 8 storey building. There were two more buildings of the same size – Eton Rise was one, Eton Hall was in the middle and Eton Close on the other end of Eton College Road, NW3.

We were whisked up in a lift to the third floor and entered Flat 91. This flat consisted of two bedrooms, a sitting room, bathroom and toilet and a kitchen. Maciej and Tota had one bedroom while I slept on a mattress on the floor in our parents' room.

After about a year, we had to change flats to No 104 but still in the same building. This flat only had one bedroom. By this time Maciej was at a Polish private school at 1920, London Road, Glasgow E2. Tota was also at a Polish school at Dunelaster House, Pitlochry, Perthshire. When these two came back to stay in the flat during the school holidays, they also had to sleep on mattresses in the sitting room of No 104. In September 1943 I was sent to a Polish school in the beautiful large house lent to the Poles by Sir Alec Douglas-Hume, later to be Prime Minister. The house was called Castlemain and was near Douglas in Lanarkshire, Scotland.

What do I remember from my first years in England? For a whole year, I was given the chance to recuperate from our ordeal and spent my time playing in the flat. My life consisted of being taken for walks to Primrose Hill, where there were swings and, as it was one of the highest points, a base for barrage balloons. They reminded me of big elephants up in the sky – whether they actually ever brought down a German plane, I doubt it. Walking with Father on Hampstead Heath, making and using a bow and arrow, running everywhere on the heath, as children do, especially at my age of eight and nine. There were many bombed out sites where wild flowers had started to grow and I was longing to jump into these and explore – but was I allowed? No. I played a lot with lead soldiers. Being a son of a General, that was not surprising! There was a whole platoon of Polish soldiers; the one with the Polish flag, which I still have, although he stands on a bit of plasticine now. There was this game called 'L'Attaque' with various ranks of soldiers made out of cardboard, each one standing on a metallic base. Somewhere or other I still have it and it is probably worth a lot of money by now if I could only find it!

A very large map of the world was pinned to a wall in the sitting room. In 1942/3 the map had many countries coloured pink. All belonged to the British Empire and Africa had the biggest number with the British names of the countries such as Nyasaland, Rhodesia and Swaziland. These names would all change in the next couple of decades.

During this period of my childhood, Father introduced me to stamp collecting. He used to bring me large envelopes packed with stamps taken off letters. I loved sorting them out, soaking them off the paper, drying them in sheets of blotting paper, then placing them in the Stanley Gibbons album. I do believe that many postcards were probably destroyed by me, wishing to get the stamps off them. Father used to make me find the countries on the large map. *"This way you will learn the geography of the world"* he said.

Much later I became a philatelist – in other words a more serious stamp collector. I wrote articles and had them printed in the Stamp Magazines. I even won a prize of £100 for one article and won first prize in a Welsh Philatelic Exhibition.

I did not have any friends in that first year but don't remember being lonely. I was rather spoilt by Mother and went everywhere with her. I was very much "Mummy's boy".

War was still all around us. Many a time the sirens screeched their hideous noise, often in the middle of the night. We raced to get to the tube station at Chalk Farm. It was rather frightening and, at the same time memorable, seeing an air raid of planes flying above in deadly combat, search lights criss-crossing the night sky and anti-aircraft guns booming and their flashes in the sky.

It is peculiar what things stay in my mind. Every time I hear the song 'J'attendrai', I can still see our old gramophone. Winding it up with a handle, putting the '78' record on, placing the arm with the steel needle onto the record and then hearing the music. Mother loved Chopin of course (a Polish composer) and so there were many records which were played over and over again. After a time the '78' records got so pit-marked from the needle that the sound became absolutely terrible.

Having gone through the trauma of being sent to the Polish school as a boarder in Scotland, I had in this time learnt to stand on my own feet – probably more likely on one foot (metaphorically speaking!) So after one year, a decision was made to send me to an English school. Obviously a good decision as it was about time that I learnt

English and was involved in the English school system. And so it was at St Louis Preparatory School, Banbury, where I managed to stand on that second foot, but it was hard for me, very hard.

To begin with, I was scared and wanted to run away - again. I will never forget that first day of 20th September 1944. The train was standing on Platform 4 in Paddington station. To be precise it was the 2.10pm GWR train, with a reserved coach for the boarders going back for the Christmas Term. Mostly the boys lived in London. So, this train was about to take me to a boarding school where a foreign (to me) language was spoken; a language of which I knew only one word – 'the'. I had seen this word many times in newspapers but I could neither pronounce it nor did I know its meaning.

The noise of the steam engine, the smell of oil, mixed with coal fumes, intermingled with fond goodbyes, last instructions from the parents of the 4-13 year old boys together with kisses and tears. Yes, I do remember my tears, and they went on for a long time into the first term. My Father told me on the station platform, 'You must be brave'.

So at precisely 2.10pm our carriage jolted, started to move out of the station and picked up speed. A last wave, faces of parents fading into the distance, then I shrank into a corner, wondering why all the other boys were chattering so much as if enjoying themselves. To me it was a cacophony of sound and my ears could not understand a word. The train finally stopped in Banbury, Oxfordshire.

During the next four years (1944-48) I would come out of my shell, learn the language and in fact win the Literary Prize in my last year with a story entitled 'Escape' about our experiences in Asia. After my initial loneliness, I made many friends. I was made captain of gymnastics and cricket, played and was given 'colours' for Rugby and Hockey. I had my nose punched in boxing and won the first prize for the best garden plot in the school grounds. I was made a 'Centurion' – a 'man of responsibility'. In the end, I loved every bit of my time there!

In London Father used to travel by car with a Polish soldier as driver. He travelled to the office of Wladystaw Roczkiewicz, President of the

Polish Republic. At first this was at 2, Bryanston Court, George Street, W2 and later in 1945 at 34 Belgrave Square, SW1, where he held the title 'Chief of the Military Household of the President of the Polish Republic'.

To put the Dembinski family in context, I must first go back a very long way but only in general rather than in detail.

The ancestors of the family came from Moravia in 1106, the family settled in the district of Krakow. The first person mentioned, in 1279, was called Warsz who was Castellan of Krakow. In the genealogical tree, he is the 1st progeny. The Dembinski's coat of arms is called Rawicz. At some point we were known as Dembina Dembinski. Now I will skip seven centuries and fifteen generations. We then come to the 16th progeny or generation . His name was Alexander. Father says this of his grandfather:

"He was in the Polish Army and took part in the November 1863 Revolution. It was a heroic but hopeless insurrection against the cruel domination of Poland by Russia. 30,000 Poles lost their lives and 150,000 were exiled to Siberia. He was murdered during this rebellion in front of his own house by a blacksmith employed on the estate. The man committed this murder in front of a drunken crowd. His wife never shed her mourning black until she died."

He had three sons: Stefan Felix, born in 1840. *"I well remember him"* says Father. *"He had a very impressive figure – tall, with an aesthetic face and wearing a black patch over his right eye. He liked to dress in different colours. He wore shoes with straight tips unlike anyone else's. He carried an ebony stick which had a bone handle. He wore a gold chain hanging from one waistcoat pocket to another. In winter he would dress in furs and wore an astrakhan hat. He was always nice to us children and always arrived with some kind of present. When I was ten years old, he gave me a special present of a silver chronometer with my own monogram on the back."*

Apparently the same 'time-piece' still kept perfect time in the 1960s. Father continues,

"At the age of 23 he joined the Polish Army to fight in the 1863 Revolution. Afterwards he went to a seminary to become a priest. After studying in Rome, he became Chaplain to a Bishop. He wrote an article about the fallibility of the Pope and the Catholic Church took him to task over his logic. He was told to publicly revoke his statement but refused to do so and was consequently removed from the Church hierarchy. As a result he became a Professor of History in a secondary school in Jaslo. Later he retired to Florence, staying at 58 via di Pinti for many years. Wherever he was, he always said the first mass of the day. He spoke and wrote in Italian. Amongst many different works, he researched and had a book published about all Polish words and phrases which originated from the Latin and Italian language. He would return every other year to Poland, visiting his many friends and relations. Before each visit he would plan his programme in great detail. This included the exact times of train arrivals and departures during his itinerary. One day, for a joke, a friend got him to the railway station too late to catch his train. He was not amused and never went to visit that friend again.

At the beginning of the 20th century, he returned to Poland. He lived there in Lwow, near his brother August (my grandfather). He came to us each Sunday for lunch. Much to our annoyance, we all had to play bridge for 10 hallers (Austrian currency) a point. On winning, he would rub his hands together and laughingly say '..and I have beaten you kids again!' "

The second son was Stanislaw Eliasz. My Father reminisced about him as follows:

"Stanislaw was the youngest of the three brothers. I remember him as a very tall, handsome and elegant gentleman with blond whiskers. His son, Alexander, was older than his sister Zdzistawa. He was a spoilt only son, but with much ability. He studied at Lwow University. We did not see him much after we discovered that all the achievements he claimed were a figment of his imagination. He went around in the company of actors, later getting a job in a bank. He died soon after the end of the first World War."

We now come to the 17th progeny, my grandfather. I never knew him; in fact when I was born in 1934, he had already been dead twenty two years (1912). August Leon Roman was born in 1843. Once again, I let my Father speak about his own father:

"My father had to join the Austrian Army at the age of 16 (Poland was under domination of Austria until 1918). In 1866 he was an officer in the Italian Campaign and later served in North Hungary. On leaving the army, he attended a mining college. Later, as many did in those days, he tried his luck at drilling for oil. He did not succeed in finding any and lost all his inheritance in this enterprise. He then tried agriculture, leasing the estates of Rostwieczko and Nowe Siolo (where my Father was born). At the age of sixty he gave up agriculture and moved to Lwow where he worked in the Feliks Insurance Office. He is buried under a massive memorial stone in a beautiful wooded hillock of Lyszakowski Cemetery in Lwow (now in Ukraine and called Lviv). He married twice. His first wife died giving birth to their daughter Zofia. Zofia had smallpox as a child. She later became a teacher and worked all her life in Jaslo. The second marriage was to Michalina Wadowska."

Zofia and Michelina lived together in Jaslo and there are many postcards from these two ladies between 1939-1945.

There is one more relative, who sounds a real character and my Father describes him as follows:

"There was a cousin of mine named Kolikst Dembinski, the son of the brother of my grandfather. From his youth he demonstrated his 'originality', especially his fondness for travel. When he finished his mining studies, he got a job with a Dutch company in Borneo and Java. He was away for many years, working in the Far East. When he returned to Poland, he did not bring anything back except a collection of monkeys of many different species.

When he finally found suitable accommodation to rent, the monkeys bombarded everyone who passed by the windows. The monkeys used to find all kinds of objects to hurl at people. After many complaints, he found it impossible to rent any rooms in the town. He moved out into the suburbs and the monkeys had to be put into cages. They were so attached to him that, as soon as he entered the room, they threw themselves into his arms and clung to his neck. His other idiosyncrasy was to drive around in his cart harnessed with dogs and he dressed in the most outlandish clothes."

So these were my Father's kindred – and an interesting lot they were! Now I will tell you about my Father's life and achievements from his birth on 30th September 1887 in Nowe Siolo near Cieszanow in Galicia, to 1st September 1939 (see photos p163). The period of WW2 and his service in the Polish Army in Poland, Hungary, France, Scotland and London, has already been told. It should be pointed out that to us children he was always Ojciec (Father), never Tata (Dad or Daddy).

His father, August, gave up his agricultural profession and moved to Lwow. This was mainly to give his three sons a better education. Stefan Jacek Dembinski, my Father, the 18th progeny and the eldest, was sent to a Higher School. At his own request he was moved to a military grammar school. By attending this type of school, it would help him to be admitted into the Military Academy. Having graduated, he was accepted in 1907 into the Marie Terese Academy and given the rank of 1st Lieutenant of the 1st Regiment of the Austrio-Hungarian Uhlans based in Lwow.

In 1914 he set out for war as a divisional staff officer. He took part in the biggest battle of the 1st World War on 28th August 1914 near Jaroslaw when the Russians defeated the Austrians. After this defeat of the Austrio-Hungarian Army, he came into contact with the members of the newly-formed Polish Army under Marshal Jozef Pilsudski (1867-1935) and immediately joined it. In 1919 he fought in Lwow as a Commander of a reserve battalion in the defence of the city. On his return to the Jozef Poniatowski regiment (cavalry), he was sent to the Wolyn front. Here he took part in the early stages of the Polish-Bolshevik war at Monowicz. Next came victorious battles capturing Luck and Sarn.

After six months at the front, he became ill with typhus and spent some time in hospital. After recovery he was sent again to the front, now as a major. His first command was of the 9th regiment of Uhlans. The fighting was against the horses' artillery of the Russian Marshall Budenny. Now a Colonel, Father took part in the last and greatest horse cavalry battle of Komarow, in which four regimental commanders were killed. For his bravery he received the highest Polish military medal – the Virtuti Militari (similar to the British VC). Kossak, the famous Polish painter of this time, depicted him on his horse by the side of a hill and in the middle of that battle. On Father's death, this painting was presented to the Polish Historical Museum in London.

He wrote about the Battle of Komarow for the 'Cavalry Review' in 1934. At the battle he was in command of the 9th Regiment of Lancers. Having translated from the original Polish version, I would like to include the whole text. Historically it is of significance, being the last cavalry battle, nearly 100 years ago at the time of writing.

"About midnight on 30th August 1920, I stopped the regiment at Tyszowce. Here I received an order from the Brigade Commander to join him at Komarow as soon as possible.

We moved off at 5am on 31st August from Tyszowce. I never thought that this day would become memorable for all time; that it would be the day on which the biggest cavalry battle of the 20th century would take place.

We had just spent two days blundering about at the back of the division. We were acting as an escort to a supply column. In those days of 1920, it was rather a muddled ramshuckle band of stores and ammunition. Travelling through torrential rain and deep mud, it was a nightmare. That was yesterday. Today was a brilliant sunny day. The mood of the soldiers was now a happy one. They sang songs and were very cheerful; happy that we were returning to where we belonged. In those times, comradeship amongst the regiments of our division was highly emotional, when luck played its part in the ups of offensive actions and the downs of retreats. In the last few days we had achieved a superiority in terms of the number of horse cavalry. This increased in us a moral superiority. It tipped the balance in our favour and against our enemy.

About 8am I reported to the Divisional Commander, Lieutenant Colonel Brzeczonski. At that moment the advance guard of the 2nd Regiment moved off towards Czesniki. Having received orders and acquainted myself with the situation, I ordered a short stop. Availing ourselves of this time, we thought of breakfast. Regretfully, it appeared that the village here had no food left. To our delight we found a plum orchard in this most attractive and hospitable village. So, as we were starving, we tucked into these plums.

These carefree moments were interrupted by shots fired from a short distance. Later, the sounds of guns firing awakened our curiosity. On the western side of the village where I was stationed, I observed through my binoculars that the 2nd Regiment of Lancers were dispersed on hilly ground around Roszczyzna. They were encountering the enemy. A few puffs of smoke from the guns appeared in the blue sky. It was time to get started and follow the brigade, which stretched itself in front of us.

A moment later, I went to orientate myself, together with my staff, about the present situation. I found the staff officers of the brigade on the hill top, south of Ruszczyzna. I immediately realised that in the nearest field there was an unequal struggle going on between a courageous but tired 2nd Regiment and some units of the 8th Regiment of Uhlans. The situation needed prompt intervention.

It only required a sharp order from Colonel Bszczonski for me to return at a gallop to my regiment. The regiment was at that time crossing a marshy valley south of Ruszczyzna. I ordered a unit of the cavalry from the right flank to position itself on the northern end of Wolica Swiatycka as an insurance precaution. I spread the regiment out in a charging formation and moved in the direction of Nowa Wolica woods.

A decisive strike at well-organised formations, closely formed enemy, necessitated hand to hand fighting. This improved the chances in our favour. All our fighting units joined the 9th Regiment of Uhlans in this strike, which took us onto the high ground south of Czesniki.

After a couple of kilometres, we met the enemy in strength. They hit us from the centre and left flank and resulted in our units being pushed down into a valley, near the southern part of Wola Swiatycka village. Here it was that the regiment reorganised itself afresh. Two companies, the third and fourth, were left as rear-guards.

A fresh enemy thrust from the West had re-ignited the battle. The regiment commenced in a charging formation for the third time. The battle was still raging in the valley bottom in the west of hill 265. The battle swung this way and that amidst horrendous roars and explosions from both our own and the enemy's artillery.

Looking at the battle scene, it reminded me of how a hare must feel when surrounded in a small hollow. The huntsmen shooting without taking aim, each missing the poor creature but instead peppering their companions' boots!

This struggle of the opposing cavalry lasted about two hours. About 11 o'clock in the morning, a critical moment arrived. The enemy brought a fresh brigade into the battle from the north-west after capturing a part of Wola Swiatycka village.

Captain Sulkiewicz's horse battery and the Commanders of the 8th and 9th Regiments of Uhlans, as well as Captain Szymanski and Lieutenant Czarnoty were sent to this village by the shortest possible route to ensure there was no way the massed enemy units could get out.

Being myself in the midst of the battle, I suddenly realised that only a few minutes later after our units got too near the village, the enemy unexpectedly retreated in a panic. The Bolsheviks deserted the field of battle after nearly two hard days of fighting.

It is possible that at the time when our strength was at its weakest, the enemy's moral resources were at its lowest ebb. This is of course a characteristic of a cavalry battle. When there is no decisive superiority of either side, it is at this precise psychological time when the moral strength wins the contest. You cannot call this outcome by any word or for that matter measure it in any way.

Having now reached the top of the hill, for which we have now been fighting for such a long time, the fighting suddenly stopped. Only loose horses ran here and there. Patrols crossed over the fields. The medics began their quiet work with their utmost devotion.

In the middle of the battle and leading my regiment for the second or third time, and charging on a favourite chestnut horse (fatally wounded later in the day), I went ahead, somewhat too far from the unit. All of a sudden, a single Bolshevik rider appeared in front of us with a pistol in his hand. My pistol came quickly out of the holster. Both of us halted facing each other at a distance of a few metres. Our right arms held the pistols at arm's length. Both of us aimed at each other's heads. Six times we exchanged shots. Six times the bullet missed its target. My lancers stopped behind me. The Russian unit stopped behind my opponent. It was only for a moment, but in this moment both observed this duel, just like two audiences. Having emptied the bullets from the pistols, the encounter was finished. Immediately my lancers leapt upon my opponent and killed him before he could unsheathe his sword. Later I found that my opponent was a Bolshevik brigade commander. Much later Romnel mentioned this incident in his book.

Our rest lasted a few minutes. The 6th Cavalry brigade was fighting near Niemirkow. Guns thundered incessantly but the bombardment was over a very large area. As the sun was receding towards the west, the brigade received an order to move in the direction of Niemirkow. My regiment, exhausted from the two days of marches and the exertion of the day's fighting, received an order to join the brigade at its rear.

As we were going up a hill, we were hidden from the view of the Czesnika-Niemirkow valley. On our left stood a battery covering one of the units of the 1st Regiment of Uhlans and its task was also to protect our march.

Riding alongside the regiment, I noticed with concern the state of our horses, which looked very exhausted to me. Suddenly I observed some kind of disturbance near the protective battery. After a moment, a lone rider detached himself from the battery. He galloped as fast as he could towards my regiment. This officer, belonging to the 1st regiment, gave me the following report. 'A huge mass of Bolsheviks are attacking straight at you', he said, indicating the direction of Nowa Wolica at our rear.

Between the enemy and ourselves was a minor fold in the land. The situation needed an immediate decision. The enemy would hit us from behind. At once I turned the regiment around and formed it into companies. One company was sent to cover the battery. This ensured it would support our flank at the same time. An officer was sent with a report to the brigade.

It must only have been seconds, but every moment the rest of the brigade distanced itself from us in the opposite direction. It occurred to me that although the regiment had fought against a superior force in the morning, we would now be faced with a final sacrifice to stop the enemy in their tracks. Hopefully, this would allow sufficient time for the rest of the brigade to notice our predicament and come to our rescue. This action could significantly affect the outcome of the whole battle.

Evaluating the exhaustion of men and horses, as well as the larger superiority of the enemy, I feared whether our tired men had sufficient moral strength. I decided to strike at the enemy in one solid body. I could rely on the officers to keep the body of men under control. The units were going in a column. In between the units went the gun carriages. The officers were bustling around in the front, inspiring courage in the Uhlans. This was how the regiment moved – at a quick pace – like a Greek phalanx in the direction of Wolica.

The patrols that were sent forward returned a few minutes later with the news of the oncoming storm. As I rode up to higher ground, the sight that manifested itself in front of me was two-fold. Firstly, the background of the setting sun and the dark violet colour of the woods – a view both threatening and wonderful. Secondly, in the foreground, an unruly multi-coloured mob, ten times superior, rushing towards us with their typical savage cries. Their swords held high, glittered in the setting sun. Single shots could be heard aimed in our direction.

Now our artillery, positioned on the hill and to the right of us, spoke their growly sounds. Machine guns fired continuously. Our luck held. The fire from the flank struck mercilessly at the ranks of the enemy. It caused them to halt their advance. This was our salvation. It gave enough time for the rest of the brigade to join us.

My regiment still rode at an ambling pace. I was saving the horses' strength until the last moment. Only when I saw the enemy a short distance in front of us did I give the command to trot. The closed ranks now rushed forward with myself in the lead. This was a unique cavalry charge. It very much depended on taking a time advantage when leading a weakened force against an enemy. This was especially true now, as the enemy had very much greater supremacy in numbers and also had a favourable lie of the land. They could have quite easily demolished our small handful in no time at all.

Evidently the guns must have stopped his energy to fight as his impetus was halted. The encounter succeeded rather by the inactivity of the two opposing sides at different times. My regiment now yielded to the overwhelming superiority of the enemy and turned back. At the same time the 8th Regiment of Uhlans led by Col Brzeczowski attacked in a great rush. This surprise threat by this famous regiment attacking the enemy from the flank, caused a complete collapse and retreat of the Bolsheviks. By the darkening dusk, the field of battle slowly became deserted.

Night arrived. The moon was shining when this battle ended. It ended as surprisingly as it began. Silence and the dusk of the night blotted out all details around us.

My regiment received an order to remain on the field of battle and shield the withdrawal of the divisions through Komarow to Tyszowiece. Riding along the left flank and the north border of Wolica Swiatycka, I hurried the regiment, patrolling its fields.

The battlefield was drowned in a mysterious dusk. It was only by moonlight that we could find our wounded and dead. In this cavalry charge, the very courageous and popular sergeant and an old legionnaire, Boleslaw Ziemba was killed. Lieutenant Wani, in spite of being concussed in the morning, and against my orders, stayed with the regiment but was grievously wounded.

So the day ended, the importance of which we later recognised. The very strong horse artillery and cavalry of the Russian Commander-in-chief Budienny, finished itself on the field at Kamarow. It would never again confront us."

* * * *

Well, now that World War One was over and Poland had become a free country after 100 years of being governed by foreigners, I can continue with my Father's career in the Polish Army.

From 1922 to 1928 he was given command of 18th Regiment of Ulhans. On 24th July 1922 he married Maria Plewkiewicz in Lubasz church near the Slawno estate of her father Jan.

From 1928 to 1930 he took over the command of the 8th Cavalry Regiment. Then in 1930 he was made Commanding Officer of the 12 cavalry brigades in Ostrolenka for another couple of years.

In 1932, now with the rank of Brigadier General, he took over the management and maintenance of the Polish military supply columns. As a cavalry officer, he was most interested in horse breeding. It should be remembered that at this time horses were still used to a great extent in the Polish Army, especially in the supply department. In the last years before the war, he was responsible for breeding Arab horses. These were exported not only to America, but also to armies of Bulgaria, Czechoslovakia, Estonia, Greece and Turkey.

The rest of his career from 1939 has already been covered previously. His decorations from both world wars were as follows:

V Class (Silver Cross) Virtuti Militari

Krzyz Waleczny (Cross of Valour) 4 times, incl Class II & IV

Gold Krzyz Zaslugi (Cross of Merit)

Grand Cross & Knights Cross Polonia Restituta (Rebirth of Poland)

Cavalier (IV class) Legion D'honneur

British Order of Bath & War Medal

Bulgarian Order of Commander (Crown)

III class Latvian Order

Estonian Cross of Merit

II Class Yugoslavian Order of Commander

II class Rumanian Order

I class Greek Cross of Merit

Having worked as Chief of the Military Household of the President of the Polish Republic from October 1941 to 1947 (see p164), he was formally demobbed. Actually the British Government no longer wanted anything to do with the Polish Government in Exile in London, and together with all military men and women, they were discarded, rather like 'unwanted furniture'!

As mentioned previously, there is no correspondence of any interest to or from Persia, Palestine and South Africa. I am sure there must have been letters, postcards or telegrams but none were kept for posterity. So we have a blank between May 1941 and December 1942. However, from this latter day, there are twenty postcards from which information can be gained, as well as several envelopes without the letters they originally contained. All the postcards from late 1942 to June 1944 were posted from Poland, still under German occupation, with the General Gouvernment stamps. All, apart from one which went via Lisbon, were sent to Borys or Helena Zaleski at Kommendors gatan 40/II, Stockholm, Sweden. Both Portugal and Sweden were neutral countries, so the German authorities allowed the post to be sent there. I rather think that the address in Stockholm must have been the Polish Consulate, who then sent them over to London, for they were certainly received there by my parents.

By 1945 the Germans had left and the Russians took over Poland. From this year the post travelled straight to London. The stamps used were very badly produced, some were without perforations and the paper was shabby in quality. Even in 1946 they were censored.

The first postcard kept from this era is postmarked 14th November 1942 from Jaslo, Distr Krakau. It is from Michalina and Zofia Dembinska. It is the first one to go via Stockholm and tells us that Father's mother, Michalina, and her stepdaughter, Zofia, have just moved to a new apartment at Ulica Mostowa 12, still in Jaslo, near Tarnow. They thank us 'from the bottom of my heart for your kindness' for sending such an expensive parcel, which arrived in excellent condition 'without being interfered with'. They say that they were reasonably alright.

On 19th February 1943 the card's sender is Michal Kuta (before the war he was Father's valet), but the card is actually written by Jozefa Plewkiewicz (Mother's mother – still living in our Warsaw house at Ulica Karwinska , Fort Mokotow). It seems strange that she uses Michal's name. Was she afraid to give her own name at this stage? Again she uses the 'post box' address (as they were called) in Stockholm, with 20 pf stamp of Adolf. An interesting letter with her latest news about everyone:

"*Dearest Marysia* (diminutive of Maria, my mother), *Everything is alright in the house. We all live together. Benigna has a good job as a housekeeper, Michal is a postman. Marynka, although lame, cooks our meals. The ground floor is let to a lady 'with a feather'. We cook downstairs.* Stefan (Plewkiewicz, Mother's brother) *remains in Slupca and has a job as a bookkeeper with a German builder. I feel much better and happier now. I have lost much weight, so I can wear Tota's clothes. I teach German so that I can earn something to live by and also as an occupation. I always have good news from Slawno. The garden here in Karwinska is looked after well. Very kindest greetings for Maciej's Saint's day. I probably won't recognise the children. In the* spring I hope to go to Slupca. I will have to work manually and hard. At the moment in Warszawa the days are nice and warm. We have heating in the house."

Next month on 19th February 1943, Benigna Czekata writes from Ulica Karwinska (you may remember the last time we saw her was at Przemysl station when she didn't succeed in joining us in the cattle wagon before being transported to Russia). Once again the letter is sent via the roundabout route to London, with the same Adolf Hitler stamp. She says that everyone was overjoyed to receive the postcard (from London – but I wonder what route that took). She continues,

"We are all well, all four of us. Granny (Jozefa Plewkiewicz, but not Benigna's granny*) keeps well, Uncle* (Stefan Plewkiewicz) *writes often. Marynka is lame – she cooks and looks after us all. We manage alright – we have enough food and one can say we lack nothing. I work for the Germans in Frascati Street* (which incidentally is the house occupied by Marie Curie and is now a museum*) in Warszawa during the day.*

She goes on to address me:

"Dear Andrzejek, write to me a few words – I presume you have learnt to write."

There is also 'sincere greetings' from Marynka Panienki.

Benigna, Marynka and Michal were called 'servants' in the pre-1940 years. They obviously were very fond of Father and Mother and us children. I believe they must have been treated as part of the family.

Onward a few months and there is another letter from Jozefa Plewkiewicz, my maternal grandmother, with some more news about their life in Warszawa:

"Everyone is working and so can keep alive. Everything is so expensive, on top of the inflation and taxation. Mrs Jachelska (the one 'with the feather' I presume) *lives with her brother on the ground floor. Not a very good choice; she complains the whole time. Stefan* (Plewkiewicz) *is still in Slupca and has a job with the magistrates. He is very lonely*

and homesick. We have not lost anything at home, only a few incidentals. Benigna brought back all the linen. The garden is lovely, only the birds are missing. The cherry trees did not die in the hard winters and produced much fruit. I have lost a lot of weight. I weigh 125 lb."

I wish she had made the comment about not losing anything in more detail, eg Uncle Stanislaw's manuscript, books, art, etc.

On 20th September 1943 there is a postcard from Zofia Dembinska from Jazlo, via Stockholm, only thanking us for a parcel received in good condition and to say they are both well.

On 27th October, Zofia Dembinska says they received a photograph of the 'children' (that's us in London) *'who are nearly grown up'*. She goes further to say: *'during these times that we are living in, we are feeling more or less alright – as you might expect from two elderly women with heart problems. My sister from Warszawa also writes quite often – unfortunately she has only visited us once a year over the past four years'.* (She means Maria (Mucha) Jakubowska, who is really her half-sister).

Talking about Mucha, the next postcard is from her written from Bohomolcia 17, Zoliborz, Warszawa via the usual route. The message is mainly about receiving parcels of sweets, clothing and sundries. The date of the postmark is 12 November 1943, and so she states that *'the hard time of winter is beginning. In the last couple of days, the weather has turned cold with a fierce and freezing wind. Everyone is walking around as if they were lame. Thank you Stefan* (Father) *for remembering me – it gives me courage to live."*

There is the last postcard from Jaslo sent via Stockholm, written on 28th December 1943, postmarked 4th January 1944. I would love to know how long it took the postcard to be sent on to London and be received there. In the letter Zofia Dembinska thanks for the sweets. She says her health is worsening. Also she writes very timidly as *"I am ashamed for what I am about to ask you. I would be delighted if you could include a used dark grey or navy skirt in the next parcel (if there is one)"*. She would never receive it. She died on 10th February 1944.

There are two postcards in 1944 from Maria Jakubowska, known as Mucha in the family. Both are sent from Jaslo, when she was visiting. Both are sent via Stockholm and with the German Eagle swastika and 'Oberkommando der Wehrmacht' censor mark. The first one is postmarked 7th March 1944 and, apart from thanking us for sending a parcel with sardines, the postcard is a very sad one. She says:

"I have to inform you and Stefan of the sad news about my sister (actually half-sister). *Zofia died on 10th February. The horrid anaemia, with which she was ill for the past years, advanced to such intensity in the last couple of months that it was impossible to help her. My old mother's* (Michalina) *health is reasonably alright. Due to her age and advanced state of sclerosis, as well as her exhausted damaged heart, she may not have long to live* (she died on 8th December 1944). *I am trying to give her everything in my power as a 'sweetening' before I have to return in a few days."*

The second postcard is postmarked 7th June 1944. She is back in Jaslo nursing her mother, Michalina Dembinska (my grandmother). She tells my parents in London:

"I received the parcel with clothes. I hope I will be able to exchange it well, as it is nice and in good style. Mummy's state of health is unchanged. Lately the temperature has suddenly changed from cold to very hot days – this has made her weaker. Otherwise our days and life in general is monotonous and quiet. We always stay at home, think, talk and even dream of you dear people. We guess what the children are doing. Today we received a parcel with warm clothes."

The last letter's envelope (no letter enclosed) from Mucha is from Krakow dated 26th January 1946 from Ulica Bandvrskieso 34. Mucha died in Krakow 20 years later so presumably she moved from Warszawa sometime in the past year.

Now let me turn to my other grandmother – Jozefa Plewkiewicz. To remind you, she was forcibly ejected from the Slawno estate and had spent the war years at our house at No 1 Karwinska street in Warszawa. Four of the postcards are from this address. The fifth is from Slupca, the village where the other estate was located, however she did not go to the estate but to live in the village. Probably the reason for going there was to be near to her son, Stefan Plewkiewicz. All four postcards from Warszawa, still under German occupation, were sent via Stockholm and hence to London.

The first one is postmarked on 12th May 1944. Jozefa writes:

"Is it as cold over there as it is in Warszawa? Strong winds, only 3-4°C. A lot of work for me in the garden and allotment; the best garden in the Fort Mokotow district. The apple trees will fruit for the first time and all the fruit trees are looking beautiful (incidentally she is now 72 years old*). We have not sold anything from the house; everything is left for my children. From the lessons I give, I have enough to live reasonably well. We all work, so we can manage. My son* (Stefan P) *writes often. He still works with the magistrates but feels very lonely."*
(His age now is 32)

The second postcard is postmarked Warschau 31.5.44 with the usual General Gouvernement Adolf Hitler stamps. Her news this time is:

"After the cold and rains, it is now Whitsun. I am sitting alone thinking of my children and grandchildren. The wisteria is flowering this year for the first time. The cold winters froze it but after pruning it has grown again. " The rest is about her friends locally, from Poznan and Slupca.

On a postcard postmarked 23rd June 1944, she writes (excerpts only):

"We have had a lot of rain lately, so at least I don't have to water the garden. Stefan is going to Bavaria. Our home has new occupants (obviously the lady with the feathers moved out!) *Probably they will stay. The parcels arrived safely – we had to pay 500 zl. I fell down the stairs from the top and twisted my ankle – it's hurting but there isn't the time to be ill. After these lessons* (in German*) that I give, my head spins."*

Her last correspondence from Warszawa is a postcard also postmarked 23rd June 1944. This is a card saying (in German) that she had received two parcels. This card is sent via Herr Leon Zawalski, Rua Alexandre Hercubaur str 41, Lisboa, Portugal.

As we have reached the year of 1944, I would now like to turn to a phase in Poland's history. Most of it is always heroic; I think the Polish National anthem encourages that heroism:

Jeszcze Polska nie zginela, pukl my zyjemy

Poland will never be forsaken as long as we are alive

The greatest act of resistance carried out by the Home Army (Armia Krajowa) was during the Warsaw Rising against the Nazis starting on 1st August 1944 when the Soviet army was posed to enter the city. The Home Army's Commander-in-Chief, Bor Komorowski (later, in the 1950s he visited my Father at our house in Clapham), believed that a Polish-led liberation of Warsaw would strike a blow against the Germans, but also legitimise the London Government-in-Exile's claim to govern Poland and 'mobilise the entire population spiritually for the struggle against Russia'. The Home Army expected that the Soviet troops would come to their aid. For two months the Red Army watched and waited on the other side of the River Vistula in Praga. Unaided, the Poles fought on in what has been described as the most heroic, and by far the bloodiest, urban insurrection that Europe has ever seen. 150,000 poorly armed men, women and children faced the full might of the Nazis. The Germans drove rows of civilians in front of their advancing troops and roped women and children to the sides of tanks to deter attacks, while artillery and air bombardment reduced the city to rubble.

"Much was due to the resourcefulness of the insurgents, to brilliant improvisations to their auxiliary service, largely run by women, scouts, and above all to their unbreakable spirit. Where AK platoons possessed only one gun for every two men, the 'night watch' would take over the

weapons of the day watch. So long as the guns of the dead and wounded could be recovered, the ratio of guns to men was actually increasing. Weapons and ammunition had often to be won from enemy stores. Communication was maintained through warrens of deep trenches and sewers. Underground kitchens, hospitals, workshops and command posts continued to function in the deep, impenetrable levels of Warsaw's multi-storeyed cellars. The men and women of the AK fought like tigers at bay, undeterred by horrendous casualties and by any hope of survival after capture."[9]

Here is an extract from Commander 'Eta' opening up the route in a sewer from the city centre to Mokotow:

"The bitter smell of hydrogen sulphate, mixed with that stagnant odour of rotting slime and mouldering plants assaulted the nostrils. The yellow, concentrated light of the lanterns fell a few metres before us, sliding along the lichen covered oval vault. The surface of the mud shone in the light like black, shiny metal. The height of the sewer did not exceed 1½ metres. We had to bend our legs at the knees to stoop even lower ..... and to rest our arms on the slippery wall.

It was not hard to guess we were under Romolo Square. To the left stretched Aleja Jerozolimska, to the right was Ulica Szuha with its dense concentration of SS men.... The sewer then became narrower and lower...

Crunch! Crash! With the jarring of iron and the cracking of crushed stone, a tank was moving over the top of us.... But then it passed. 'It isn't even worth trying under Ulica Pulawska' my companion remarked.....The whole area could have remained in enemy hands.

The mud stuck to our legs. Sultry weather, lack of expertise and failure to conserve strength intensified the exhaustion. We had to crawl. We groaned from fear ...It would only take a shower of rain to block the exits and drown us...we had to slither on elbows and knees holding our breath.

---

[9] 'Rising '44' by Norman Davies

A catchment chamber. We could sit on the bottom, straighten our backs and rest, but the manhole above was closed....where were we? At the next chamber it was the same story. The sewer stretched on and on. Our strength was spent. We could not get out and we would not make it back.

There was no way of understanding how it happened. An impossible draught of cool air revived us. We noticed a pale glow like a half moon in the sky. Swiftly we made for the metal climbing irons. Up and up we climbed. I raised my head above the surface. No light, not a living soul.

'Stuj! Renki do gory!' (Stop, hands up!)

My tension eased. They are ours.

'From the City Centre' I cried 'From Commander Monter' "[10]

Where this 2nd Lieutenant entered this sewer in Mokotow, he would have been near our house at 2, Ulica Karwinska. Our grandmother, Jozefa Plewkiewicz, would have been there during this time. She was living there throughout the whole war, together with Benigna, Marynka and Michal – our servants up to September 1940. When visiting the house, I remember seeing a plaque nearby commemorating persons who were killed during the Rising of '44.

Father's sister Maria (Mucha) Jakubowska lived at Bohomolca 17 in the Zoliborz district in Warszawa. Zoliborz is north of the centre and there was much fighting there as well.

The Warsaw Rising ended after six weeks in defeat and the deaths of 245,000 inhabitants. Hitler ordered that the city should be 'razed without trace' and those buildings which remained were dynamited. 700,000 survivors were transported to forced labour and concentration camps. When the Soviet Army finally entered the gutted city in January 1945, over 90% of its buildings were destroyed, later to be magnificently rebuilt exactly as they looked before.

---

[10] 'Rising '44 by Norman Davies

Following in the footsteps of the victorious Red Army came a new government called the Committee of National Liberation, formed in Moscow, led by a Communist. The NKVD or Secret Police soon imprisoned members of the AK into concentration camps and their leaders were put on trial as 'saboteurs and subversionist bandits'. By the time peace was declared in May 1945, the whole of the country lay under Soviet rule, and the Soviet army was to remain on Polish soil for over forty years.

The population of Poland had fallen by nearly one third. In 1939 it was 34.5 million; in 1945 it was 23.9 million.

I don't know when my grandmother, Jozefa Plewkiewicz, decided to move from living in our house in Warszawa to Slupca. There is an envelope postmarked 3rd October 1945. The Germans had by now been defeated, it was the Communist regime which now issued 'Poczla Polska' stamps and these were used for some time. The sender's address on the back is ul 3 Maja, Konin Parish, Slupca. This is the first letter or postcard that was received in London since June 1944 (addressed to Maria Dembinska, 34 Belgrave Square, London – the President's office where Father worked).

The next envelope from Jozefa, with no letter, was postmarked 7 December 1945. This time the sender's address is changed to Ulica Poznanska 12, Konin Parish, Slupca. It looks as if she had moved to the same house/flat as her son, Stefan.

The last postcard was postmarked 25th May 1946 from the same address in Slupca to 104, Eton Hall, London NW3. I will let the message tell its own story:

"*Dear Maryzia* (Maria Dembinska), It is a very long time since I have heard from you. This makes me worried. Thank you sincerely for the parcel. The shoes fit perfectly, also for the skirt, blouse, scarf and knickers. I am more than happy to get all these, as they are all needed. I am still working in the Co-op (She is now aged 74). The wages are not very good. I don't have to think much while I am working. I am *hoping to go to Warszawa for a couple of days. I can't go for longer as I can't get more holiday. I was so happy to get a card from Andrzej. I cannot understand how this youngster can already write so well. Is Tota studying medicine? We are having a drought here. The nights are cold, often frosty. I wish I was with you all."*

Jozefa Plewkiewicz died the following year in Slupca on 5th May 1947.

The last postcards are from Stefan Plewkiewicz (Mother's brother). All are from Slupca, where he had been living and working during the German occupation and since then under the Polish but pro-Russian government.

The first card is postmarked 19th December 1945. It is really like a Christmas card sending 'Madame Plewkiewicz' *(why use Mother's maiden name?)* happy greetings. He says he still works as a researcher in the accounts department and says that they (he and his mother) are both well.

The next card is postmarked 18th February 1945. It tells that they received the three parcels. "*The trousers are fine for me, the scarf I really love."* He says that his mother is well and that she has been to Poznan (at one time her husband, Jan Plewkiewicz, used to own one of the houses in the main market square in Poznan). She met up with her friends. He says that when the weather improves, she will go to Warszawa and probably to Slawno as well. "*Slawno still has not been divided"* (by the Russians of course, who loved to divide all estates and give the land to the local 'peasants' who then did their best to mismanage the assets, resources, stock and property).

The third postcard, postmarked 2nd March 1946 has the following interesting requests from Stefan: *"My spectacles have gone wrong. At the moment I can't get new ones. The lenses are strong, like yours. Please send to me if it's possible. I would also like a fountain pen if it is not too expensive over there. It would be wonderful to have one."*

The last postcard is postmarked 17th May 1946. They had received another parcel and complained that they have not had news for a long time. He says, *"During the spring, I will go to find some fresh country air, which will be good for my nerves, away from the town of Slupca."* (He was 34 in 1946).

Some time later he married Wanda Smuszkewicz. They had four children – Maciej, Krystyna, Ewa and Olek. He died in Slupca on 26th August 1965, aged 53.

CHAPTER 9

SETTLING IN OUR ADOPTED COUNTRY

1945 ONWARDS

This chapter will deal with the end of the Second World War in 1945. It will concentrate on the fate of Poland and therefore of its soldiers and civilians who had arrived in Britain.

The synopsis of this era is excellently presented in the book "Keeping the Faith, the Polish Community in Britain" by Tim Smith and Michelle Winslow. Much of the content in this section is extracted from it.

"The War had brought deep and lasting changes to Poland, ruled over by a Soviet-backed regime. Post-war Europe had been drawn up by the 'Big Three' Allied powers – Churchill, Roosevelt and Stalin – at the Conference of Tehran (1943) and Yalta (1945). The Americans and British had bowed to Stalin's demands. With the defeat of the Germans, Poland was moved bodily 150 miles to the West. Although the 'Recovered Lands' in the west of this new Poland had been taken from Germany, half of the Poles' pre-war territory had been incorporated into the Soviet Union, including the cities of Wilno and Lwow. Polish communities in those eastern areas were expelled from the Soviet Union to repopulate the towns in Poland and the Recovered Lands from which the German inhabitants had been removed".

Let a Polish airman, who fought in the Battle of Britain give his views:

"Settlement in Britain was made all the more difficult by our feeling of betrayal. The treaties signed by the three powers seemed, especially to those who'd served in the British services, as a betrayal. We felt extreme bitterness towards our allies, who recognised the puppet Polish

government, which was killing people who'd fought for our country. The withdrawal of recognition of the legitimate Polish Government-in-Exile in London was a bitter blow. We didn't trust our allies anymore and it didn't help us to settle."

At the end of the War, the rest of Europe was awash with people displaced from their home. Over a million were Poles. They included members of the Polish forces, refugees who had fled the Nazi or Soviet armies via the Middle East, Africa, Italy – some soldiers, many civilians who escaped the deportations to Asia (like ourselves) coming some of the way with 'Anders Army'. These were the majority who finally settled in Britain."

A Polish woman describes how she arrived in England:

"We stayed a few months in Italy, waiting for transport to England. There were thousands of people there, families. A lot came from the west through Russia. They congregated there and everybody was waiting. I went to a special camp for families and waited there. My husband was sent to Napoli because there was officers' transport going to Glasgow, and they agreed to take him. We went by train to Calais, where we boarded a ferry to Dover. Then they took me to a camp in Horsham."

All Poles abroad feared – with justification – that they would be viewed as enemies of the Communist regime should they return to Poland. Most already had first-hand experience of Stalin's prisons and labour camps. Most war trials in Moscow of Polish military and political leaders for 'offences against the law of the Russian Republic' were widely publicised in the West, while other Polish officials simply disappeared. Deciding where to go was a long and painful process, particularly for those whose families were still in Poland. Pressure built up in émigré circles. To go back could be seen as a vote for the new regime in Poland and a betrayal of the nationalistic cause. Eventually 105,000 Polish soldiers did return to Poland. The rest settled in the West, mainly in the USA and Canada. 140,000 made Britain their home in spite of the efforts of the British (Labour) government to persuade them to go back to Poland. The Labour administration withdrew recognition from the Polish government-in-exile in London and supported the Warsaw Communist government.

A Polish soldier, now demobilised says:

"A lot of people who did go back to Poland…….. you never heard about them. They were shot or sent off to Siberia. So a lot of people were in fear of going back home. Also, there was a lot of guilt …families that had been left behind in much poorer circumstances. My mum's area that she came from, they owned quite a lot of land. Well, that was all collectivised, so it no longer belonged to her family. Her mother was left in terribly reduced circumstances. Economically, it wasn't such a good idea. Politically, it would have been suicide for a lot of them."

"Feelings of despair, humiliation and anger were further compounded when, in an effort by the British government to appease Stalin, the Polish army was deliberately excluded from the London Victory Parade held on the 6th June 1946."

"Military units from Italy arrived in 1946, followed by troops from Germany and the Middle East iin 1947 to be joined by their dependents and other civilians. The British government recognised that far from being an awkward problem, the Poles could represent a vital labour force."

"Polish ex-servicemen already in Britain found attitudes towards them changed with the ending of the War. Once British forces were demobilised, the sight of Poles, still in uniform, provoked a widespread response of 'Why don't you go home?' Despite the shortage of manpower, they were also seen as a threat to British jobs."

A Pole, who had been trained as an engineer, complained:

"I was refused a job because I was Polish. I specialised on a milling machine and I went to Laycrete for a job. They gave me a job straight away, but not on a milling machine. I say 'Why not a milling machine?' and the foreman say 'We will have a strike, because you are a foreigner.'

"Demobilisation of the Polish troops was seen as a priority and the Polish Resettlement Corps was created as a transitional stage to civilian life in Britain, providing accommodation, English tuition and training. After two years of an ordered camp life, the Poles had to move into the civilian world. They were initially restricted to working in agriculture, coal-mining, textiles, hotels, construction and the steel industry. Most found themselves in jobs completely alien to them. Those who had arrived with professional experience (apart from doctors and pharmacists whose qualifications were recognised) had to take on manual jobs. These problems were added to those of a strange language and culture. Leaflets entitled 'To help you settle in England' were produced by the Ministry of Labour. It included advice on queuing, using the word 'sorry' and dissuading men from kissing a woman's hand."

A Polish officer, who had been living in a Nissen hut in one of the camps tells us:

"It was lovely. I was so happy. We had an officers' mess, so we went to lunch and for breakfast and supper. And it was such a social life because it was all together. And suddenly after two years they said, 'Finish, no more army, now you have to disappear into the English community and do whatever you like'. And it was very hard. Everything was on the ration you see, and now we are civilians, what to do? We didn't know the language."

The problem of communication, which means learning English, is put succinctly by one Pole:

"The Polish people here, with a few exceptions, didn't see any need in learning the English language in the very beginning. Maybe they didn't have the opportunity. If you are a miner, or if you work in textiles, in dust and noisy conditions, who do you talk to? To nobody, you talk to yourself. Then when you come home to your Polish wife or husband, you converse in the language which is the easiest for you. I think it is also true that some Poles lived with the hope that one day, sooner or later, they would return to Poland."

It must have been so difficult for the men, who were moved from one place to another without much of the necessary English:

"I started to work in Leighton Buzzard and Bedford. Then I arrived to Newbury. From there I moved to Leicester, then to Sheffield. At first it was manual, not very nice jobs. They used to send us to the mines, brickyards, agriculture and things like that. But eventually, when we learnt English, we started moving up and taking other positions."

Mostly they did learn to speak English. There were others who obstinately would not. Back in 1952, I started in the hotel industry. I also had a manual job. It was at Grosvenor House Hotel in Park Lane, London in the 'Plate Room' as it was called then. Actually it was piling dirty plates, coming out from the Restaurant, into huge plate-washing machines – I only managed this job for 3 weeks. Four years later, I would be working as a waiter in that Restaurant. Coming to the point – the old men who were working in that hot and sweaty place were Polish generals, colonels and other officers who never learnt to speak English. They were stuck in these manual jobs probably till they died.

Food was another problem. When I went to the St Louis School in Banbury as a boarder, I had difficulty in dealing with English food such as Lancashire Hotpot, stewed cabbage, onion sauce, stewed lamb/mutton (mostly fat/gristle) porridge and other such delicacies.

Here is another boy talking about his time at school:

"They gave me food I never had in my life like 'beans on toast' – it's no good."

And in the 1980s, a son talking about his mother:

"Even now after forty years, she doesn't speak that much English. She depended on us. I was five and I couldn't speak English until I went to school. I can remember very early on taking over letter writing, administration, everything."

As soon as we arrived in Britain in 1942, my Mother had a private tutor to teach her English. Both she and my Father spoke and wrote English very well, but of course with an accent that defined them as foreigners.

"The early hope of a short exile, followed by a triumphant return to the homeland, was unfulfilled. Poles were to live in Britain longer than they could ever have imagined. Despite this, the aims of the community remained remarkably consistent, while the Communist regime in Poland was intent on destroying Polish society, these exiles would maintain and develop Polish culture and foster independent political thought. They would support struggles by the Church and non-Communist intellectuals within Poland itself. They helped to preserve and carry forward the nation's history and its collective memory, and thereby become the voice of an independent Poland."

Soldiers who wanted to return to Poland had this to say:

"I wanted to go back, but friends said 'For goodness sake don't go back because you will be arrested there. If you go there and they know you escaped from the Russians, they will take you to jail and they will send you to Russia.' I didn't go back at all. I have never been back."

And another:

"My friend went back and he told me, 'I write to you a little. No matter what I put to you in the letter. If I write by ink, come back. If I write by pencil, don't.' He didn't write by ink or pencil. He was locked up straight away, so I changed my mind and didn't go."

"By the end of 1949, the vast majority of Poles who were to settle here had already arrived in Britain. A Home office report estimated members at around 162,000 people, the majority being former deportees to the Soviet Union. The Polish Resettlement Act, passed by the British Government in 1947, acknowledged that the Poles were here to stay, and allocated roles for the Ministry of Labour, Health, Education and Pensions in providing for their needs and assisting

assimilation. The Polish community saw their Polishness as something to be preserved and to maintain their Polish identity.

A national network of clubs and organisations was set up. Some, such as the Polish Ex-Combatants Association (SPK) remain popular with the older generation to this day. Others, such as the Polish scouts were aimed at the younger generation. By 1960 there were some 150 Polish schools, which instilled in children a sense of pride in their roots through Polish history, literature and traditions, and attended by about 5000 children. A wealth of publications was also produced by the community. In the 1940s, the Dziennik Polski (Polish Daily) had a circulation of 3500 copies. Today it is a weekly newspaper still to be obtained."

Poles were registered as 'aliens'. They received a Certificate of Registration (Aliens Order 1920) booklet. This stated in the front, "You must produce this certificate if required to do so by any Police Officer, Immigration Officer or member of His Majesty's forces acting in the course of duty." They had to pay one shilling for this certificate. Each person had to visit the nearest police station each time they changed their address or employment.

I happen to have my Father's Registration Certificate No A225330 (see p.171-2). He registered at Piccadilly Place W1 on 25th October 1948. His details mention that he has 'No occupation', living at 19 Kenwyn Rd, SW4. His arrival in the UK was on 26.6.40 from Paris, France, that he joined the Polish forces on 1.11.18, joined the Polish Resettlement Corps on 23.10.46 and that he was discharged (as in 'demobbed') on 23.10.48. In his booklet there is just one Change of Occupation where it states "notified change of occupation to Cabinet Maker from 16.1.56 at Business Address: Baxter & Sons, 193 Fulham Road, SW3. The change was entered by the Clapham Metropolitan Police on 25.01.56. There is a stamp at the end of the booklet: "Aliens Order 1960. The holder is Exempt from Registration with the police but should retain this certificate." He also had a National Identity

Card which had to be produced on demand by a 'police officer in uniform or member of HM Armed Forces in uniform on duty'.

I had a similar Certificate; there were quite a few changes of occupation on my inside pages. Unlike my Father and Mother or sister, I became naturalised, ie a citizen of the United Kingdom, on 21st December 1960 (as Registered by the Home Office).

To ensure that I did not forget where I came from, Ojciec (Father) organised a Polish course by correspondence. I was given certain books dealing with Polish literature and history. I had to read certain sections and once a month answer questions. These used to be marked and sent back to me. Being at that time a boarder, educated through the English public school system, I found it very difficult to reconcile the one with the other. Let us say I found so many other things in life more pleasant to do than to work at those Polish lessons. Father was not happy with my extra-curricular results.

During holidays in London, I was made to join the Polish Scouts. I remember I went to Kensington Gardens, where the scout groups met all dressed in khaki shorts and shirts with a black and red neckerchief. I found it hard to associate with Polish boys. By this time I was already very well integrated with English culture and friendships. I was absolutely furious when Father made me go to a Polish scout camp, somewhere in Surrey. We camped in tents, did night exercises, played football. Actually, I enjoyed the experience, but did not repeat it.

Ojciec gave me two books in Polish to read, both by the most famous literary authors. One was actually a set of twelve books. I remember thinking 'How can I get through these!' The odd thing was that, having started on the first one, I read the rest in a very short time. These were the magnificent trilogy: "With Fire and Sword", "The Deluge" and "Pan Michal" by Henryk Sienkiewicz. This masterpiece dealt with life in the seventeenth century when the wars took place against Swedish invaders. Sienkiewicz is known in the west as the author of 'Quo Vadis' about Roman life under Emperor Nero.

The second book was of verse – "Pan Tadeusz" by Adam Mickiewicz. Published first in 1844 in Paris, it is about Lithuania of the 19th century. This epic and most prized work is about the Lithuanian plains and forests, brooks and the life of the peasantry. I see that on the title page, Father has written "Andrzejowi od Ojca, Borze Narodzenie (Christmas) 1959". At the age of 25, married with a one year old daughter and working many hours in the hotel business, I looked at this poetic masterpiece, all in Polish, then counted the pages – 330 ! Now at the age of 79, the book is here in front of me as I write. I promised Ojciec that I would read it. I have to now honour my promise after 54 years.

Referring back to 'change of occupation to cabinet maker', this must have been rather a nasty come-down for my Father. One day he is a Major General and the next a cabinet maker! Obviously he was trained well by Messrs Baxter & Sons because he became very adept not only at restoring old Queen Anne furniture, which we had in our 'salonik' in Clapham, but he used to spend hours up in his 'shop' (as we used to call it!) – his workshop. This was a shed-like structure on the second floor in the house in Clapham. I can still smell the distinctive odour of the carpenter's glue being warmed up on a small electric appliance. He used to make small tables, side tables, which became very useful for us when we first bought our house in Greenford. He also took up upholstery, buying old chairs and armchairs and re-upholstering them to look as new. With a colleague of his, he tried his hand at growing mushrooms (on a large scale) somewhere in a disused building in Kent. It wasn't a great success.

Together with his collection of lithographs, it kept him occupied for the rest of his life at home. Both my parents had a good social life. Father belonged to the ex-combatant associations, including being the honorary president of the Cavalry 8th Regiment. Both parents used to visit the 'Ognisko (Hearth) Polskie' in Princes Gate, London for meetings, lunches with other officers, diplomats and aristocrats. I remember going there for a Chopin (who else, being a Polish composer?) recital, dances and satirical evenings (the satire I used to find very difficult to understand). There was also the Polish Institute and Sikorski History Museum, of which Ryszard Dembinski was its Chairman for 40 years.

All the Polish intelligentsia used to congregate for coffee and cakes at the Daquise Restaurant next to South Kensington Underground station.

Religion had always provided the backbone of the Polish Community. Even during the war, there was the Roman Catholic Church (St Andrzej Bobola, Devonia Road– my patron saint) in London. The Masses there were attended by hundreds. Brompton Oratory among others always had a Polish Mass.

The original settlers, like my parents, believed that one day they would be able to return to an independent Poland. Relatively few of the first generation lived long enough to see the collapse of Communism in 1989. Going back to the time when my Father and his group were about to cross the Hungarian border on 18th September 1939, he took with him some Polish soil. He did not live to see Poland's freedom and return the soil. He died in Ealing, London on 26th March 1972 at the age of 85.

From about 1993, Tota, Maciej and I started proceedings with a Polish solicitor in Warszawa to get back the Karwinska house as our inheritance. I must state here and now that it was mainly Tota's initiative and hard work and, to some lesser extent, to Maciej's that we finally came to a 'settlement', for that's what it was eventually. The solicitor we first engaged was not earning his money. All expenses were of course shared by the three of us. We kept sending him money but three years went by and nothing was being done to any satisfaction.

Finally in 1996 Tota and Maciej went to Warszawa and had a showdown with this solicitor and he was 'given the boot'. A second solicitor was engaged and we very soon realised that it would be a very lengthy and complex struggle to get the house returned from the Polish Government. This new solicitor suggested that if we handed over the deeds of the house to him, thereby foregoing our inheritance, he would then hope to obtain ownership of the house himself. For this he offered to pay us 'a reasonable sum' which was a fraction of the value of the house. Maciej would not budge as he maintained that we should not give in but obtain our inheritance in full, ie the possession of Karwinska. Both Tota and I disagreed, knowing firstly how long it would take, the stress involved and the escalating costs. So Maciej was outvoted by 2:1, we handed the solicitor the deeds and he (magnanimously) handed over in dollars just over $200,000. After the expenses had been deducted, I personally received a cheque in July 1996 for £40,731. I was quite happy with this result, ending the saga of this whole business.

On 7 July 1939, two months before the war, our Father bought two parcels or plots of land. Once again Tota tried to see whether we could get back this land from the authorities. It soon appeared that the land had now been built on. The plots were both on the outskirts of Warszawa and the two plots were called "Parcelle Lesna Wola" – as 'lesna' means forest/wood, we must presume that it was just that in 1939. Wola is in the north-west of the city.

The Plot No 297, measured 1807 m^2. The house built on it has the address, Ulica Pulna 30 and was owned by Jozef Macierzynski who had bought the plot illegally giving reason that he had lived on the land. Both plots were bought by Stefan Dembinski, our Father. The aforementioned plot was for Maciej and myself, the other was for Tota. The second plot, No 297A, is now Ulica Jalowcowa 30, owned by Banski.

I still have the architect's original drawings from 7 July 1939 showing exactly where the plots were. Well, it was a good try by my sister Tota but somewhat late in being able to do anything about them. To take them to court would have taken much patience, a great deal of money and an incalculable amount of stress. Taking this matter to Polish solicitors and Polish courts would have been a very drawn out process.

At the time of Stefan Dembinski's death in 1972, there were seven Dembinski's still alive out of the 14 when this story began on 1st September 1939.

Matka (Mother) lived on in their house at 322 Windmill Road, W5. She had two strokes and spent her latter years at Nazareth home in Finchley, being looked after by nuns. She died on 22nd November 1984. Both she and my father are buried in the Ealing Cemetery in London.

Wlodzimierz and Krystyna Dembinski lived at 43 Carmenia Road, SW7. I regret I do not have the dates of their deaths. Their son, Ryszard, died in London on 29th June 2008 and is buried in Rogalin, near Poznan, Poland.

Antonina Okalow-Zubkowska (Tota), my sister, lived next door to my parents at 320 Windmill Road, W5. At the time, she and her husband Konstanty (Kostek) had their own Polish delicatessen in London. They had two children – Monika and Marek. They moved to Cambridge to be near Monika around 1998 and it is there that Tota died of leukaemia on 10th January 2004. She is buried in the same plot as my parents in Ealing Cemetery. Kostek, at the time of writing, still lives in Cambridge.

Maciej Dembinski, my older brother, graduated with a BSc (London Univ) in Middlesborough. He became an Associate Member of the Institute of Mechanical Engineers. He married Dorothy Girgis and they then moved to Canada. There he attained the position of Managing Director in Montreal, travelling to Brazil and India advising mainly on bridge construction. He lived in the same house he bought when first arriving at Pierreponds, Montreal in 1952. They had three children: Stefan, Nina and Aldona. Maciej died in Warsawa in October 2014, aged 88.

And that leaves me.....

On leaving the Jesuit public school of Beaumont College in Old Windsor, Berkshire in 1952, I chose a career in agriculture. Having obtained a place at the Shuttleworth Agricultural College, I had to work on a farm for a year. I regret to say that, having spent three months on a farm near Tetbury, I decided that farming was not for me. Returning to London, I applied for a three year Hotel Management course at Battersea College of Technology, which I started in September 1953. The course, with all the Certificates and Diplomas, was completed in July 1956.

I then spent the next years gaining experience in London Hotels, as well as in Switzerland, in the kitchen, restaurant and reception departments. During this time, in 1958, Judith Sansom and I were married in London. The next step was management at the Kistor Hotel in Torquay for four years.

In 1964 I bought a restaurant in Chichester. This was not a great success and soon I turned to teaching, starting in Torquay, followed by Cambridge, then to Oxford and from there to Fiji in the South Pacific. My last 12 years of teaching was spent at Haverfordwest in Pembrokeshire.

Anna was born in 1958 while in London, Paul while we lived in Paignton in 1961 and Simon in Chichester in 1964.

I retired in 1989 and moved to Reading. I was still working part-time until 1996, mainly in garden centres, and from this time on, enjoying walking in the countryside. In 2003 we decided to move to Carterton, Oxfordshire to be near Simon and our grandchildren. In 2014 we returned to live in Preston, Paignton, shortly after Simon had moved there.

On 2nd November 2011, I was unexpectedly given an Honorary Degree of Bachelor of the University of Surrey. This sounds very important but actually it's a bit comical. When I left Battersea College of Technology in 1956, it was never considered a university. However, a few years later, the Hotel Management course did become a degree course when it moved to the University of Surrey. They obviously thought that, 55 years later, they would give us this belated honorary degree. No doubt the belief underlying this was that there was money to be made from these new 'Bachelors', thinking that they would leave donations to the University in their wills.

So endeth my story for whom it may concern.

Andrzej Dembinski

Wedding of Stefan Dembinski and Maria Plewkiewicz (Author's parents) at Slawno 25.07.1922

Slawno in the 1930s (Author's Grandparents' estate)

Slawno in March 1993 (then used as Council Offices)

No.1 Karwinska, Mokotow, Warsaw (built in 1930s)
Views from front and rear
Photographs taken in 1993 when it was then the Estonian Embassy

General Stefan Dembinski with Medals including: Virtuti Militari, Polonia Restituta, Order of Bath and Legion d'Honneur and as Horseman and Chef d'Equippe of Polish Team at Rome Olympics 1936

General Stefan Dembinski as Commander of Army Camps, Rothesay, Scotland, 9th September 1941

General Stefan Dembinski with President of Polish Republic and Sir Howard Kennard at Union Jack Club, London, 20th June 1944

QE1 - The ship we sailed on from Port Said to Cape Town

Stratheden - The ship we sailed on from Cape Town to Liverpool, arriving 25 September 1942.

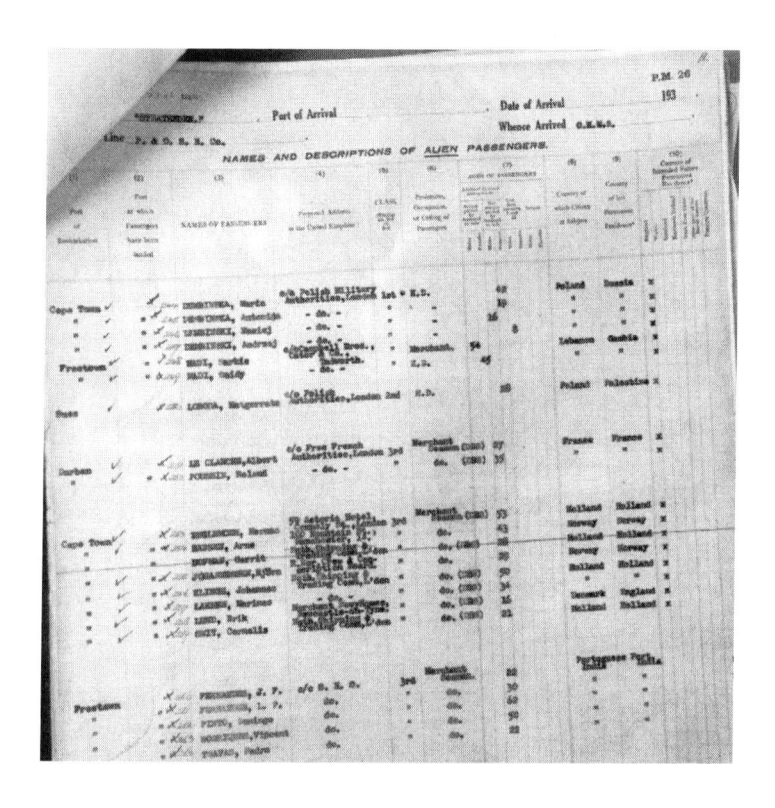

The family's names on the Stratheden passenger list.

Above - the whole family in Britain 1943
Below - Maciej, Tota and Ryszard 1943

Above: Stefan, Maciej, Aunt Krzysia, Tota, Mother (Maria) with Nina, Dorothy, Uncle Wlodzimierz, 1950s
Below: Maria Dembinska (Author's mother) at Kew Gardens, 1960s?

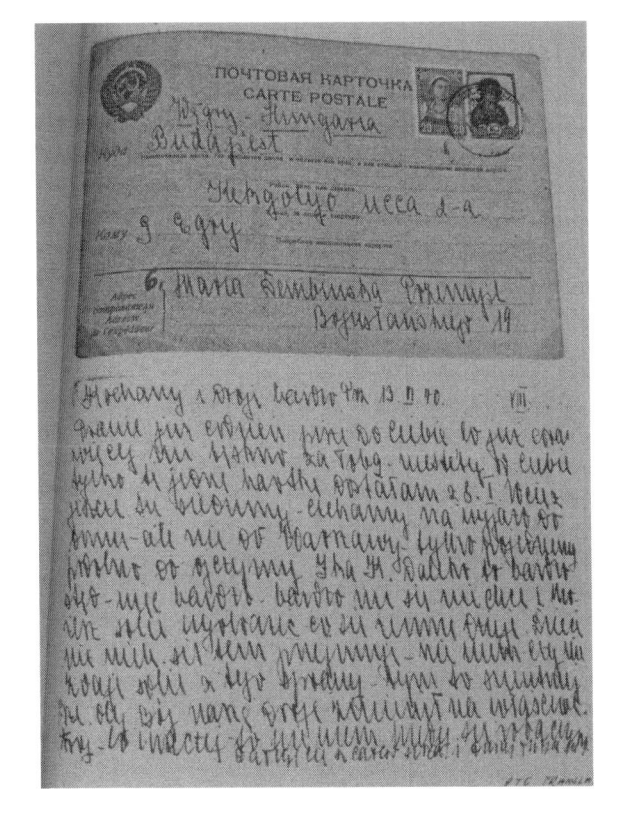

Postcard from Maria Dembinska to her husband Stefan

Dear Stefan
I write nearly every day to you because I miss you more and more. Unfortunately I have received only one postcard from you dated 28 January. We are still here waiting to go home, but not to Warsaw. We will go probably to the Fatherland of Gregory.* It is a very long way from here so I am not very keen on this to say the least. The children are not worrying, why I don't know. It is a sorry state of affairs. If only God could point us in the right direction, otherwise I don't know when we shall see each other again.
        Many kisses, your Marysia

*Code: Mother knew we were to be sent to Russia. This was two months before the journey actually took place. This was a revelation to Tota and Maciej 50 years later when these postcards were read again.

Postcard from Jozefa Plewkiewicz (living in our house in Warsaw) to her daughter Maria Dembinska

Dearest Marysia
Everything is alright in the home, we all live together. Benigna has a good job as a housekeeper, Michal is a postman. Marynka, although lame, cooks our meals. The ground floor is let to a lady with a feather. We cook downstairs. Stefan (her son) *remained in Slupca and has a job as a bookkeeper with a German builder. I feel much better and happier now. I have lost much weight, so I can wear Tota's clothes. I teach German so that I can earn something to live by and also as an occupation. I always have good news from Slawno. as on 5th July* (anniversary of husband's death in 1939?) *The garden here in Karwinska Street is looked after well. Mr and Mrs Zablocki are both in Warsaw. Very kindest greetings for Maciej's saint's day. I probably won't recognise the children. In the spring I hope to go to Slupca. I will have to work manually and hard. At the moment in Warsaw the days are nice and warm. I hope we have seen the last of the cold weather. We have heating in the house.*
Jozefa

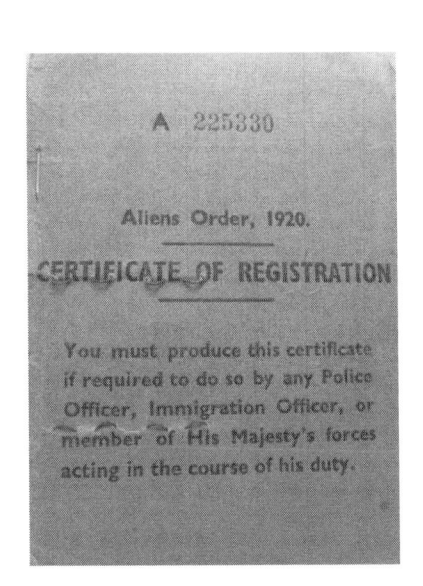

Stefan Dembinski's Alien's Order Certificate of Registration

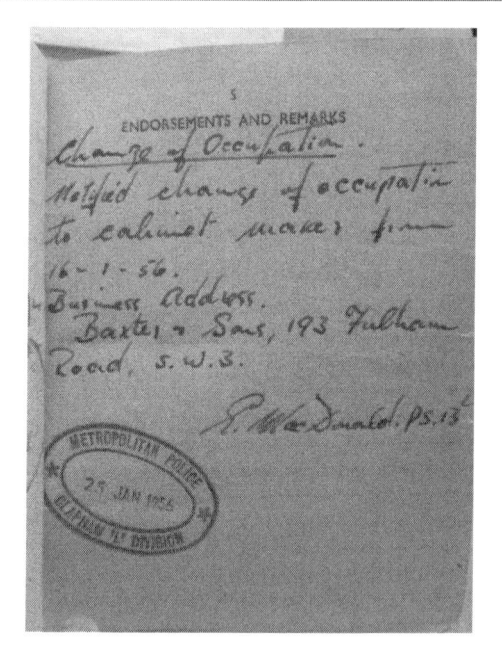

Inside the Alien's Order Certificate of Registration –
comments about change of occupation

Maciej, Tota and Andrzej outside Ely Cathedral, late 1990s

Printed in Great Britain
by Amazon